"Beatty and Cochran's *Writing the Annota* [...]
students, faculty, and librarians alike. It sh[...]
tion and on every writing center tutoring table. Instructors of research courses,
whether at the high school, college, or graduate school level, will find this book
invaluable. Any student who has struggled through writing an annotated bibliography in the past will appreciate the tips in this book that will allow them to work
much more efficiently, even joyously."

Rebecca Day Babcock, William and Ordelle Watts Professor,
University of Texas of the Permian Basin

WRITING THE ANNOTATED BIBLIOGRAPHY

This comprehensive and practical guide covers the elements, style, and use of annotated bibliographies in the research and writing process for any discipline; key disciplinary conventions; and tips for working with digital sources.

Written jointly by a library director and a writing center director, this book is packed with examples of individual bibliography entries and full bibliography formats for a wide range of academic needs. Online resources include sample bibliographies, relevant web links, printable versions of checklists and figures, and further resources for instructors and researchers.

Writing the Annotated Bibliography is an essential resource for first-year and advanced composition classes, courses in writing across the disciplines, graduate programs, library science instruction programs, and academic libraries at the secondary level and beyond. It is suitable for both undergraduate and graduate students and for researchers at all levels.

Luke Beatty is Library Director and Assistant Professor of Library and Information Science at Illinois College, USA. Luke has an MLIS and an MEd from the University of Western Ontario.

Cynthia A. Cochran is Associate Professor of English and Director of the Campus Writing Center at Illinois College, USA. Cindy has an MS in Education from the University of Illinois and a PhD in English from Carnegie Mellon University.

WRITING THE ANNOTATED BIBLIOGRAPHY

A Guide for Students and Researchers

Luke Beatty and Cynthia A. Cochran

Routledge
Taylor & Francis Group

NEW YORK AND LONDON

First published 2021
by Routledge
52 Vanderbilt Avenue, New York, NY 10017

and by Routledge
2 Park Square, Milton Park, Abingdon, Oxon, OX14 4RN

Routledge is an imprint of the Taylor & Francis Group, an informa business

© 2021 Taylor & Francis

Library of Congress Cataloging-in-Publication Data
Names: Beatty, Luke, author. | Cochran, Cynthia A., author.
Title: Writing the annotated bibliography : a guide for students & researchers / Luke Beatty, Cynthia A. Cochran.
Description: New York, NY : Routledge, 2020. |
Identifiers: LCCN 2020001038 (print) | LCCN 2020001039 (ebook) |
ISBN 9780367408879 (hardback) | ISBN 9780367408862 (paperback) |
ISBN 9780367853051 (ebook)
Subjects: LCSH: Bibliography–Methodology.
Classification: LCC Z1001 .B395 2020 (print) | LCC Z1001 (ebook) |
DDC 010/.44–dc23
LC record available at https://lccn.loc.gov/2020001038
LC ebook record available at https://lccn.loc.gov/2020001039

ISBN: 978-0-367-40887-9 (hbk)
ISBN: 978-0-367-40886-2 (pbk)
ISBN: 978-0-367-85305-1 (ebk)

Typeset in Bembo
by Swales & Willis, Exeter, Devon, UK

DEDICATIONS

Luke Beatty

- To my family and loved ones: thank you so much for all your support.
- To my friends: thank you for putting up with me.
- To my wonderful pets, past and present: thank you for spending some time with me over the years.
- To Dire Straits, Leo Kottke, I Mother Earth, and Tom Verlaine: thank you for providing the soundtrack to this book.
- To Cindy Cochran: thank you for writing this book with me (even though you wanted to write another one).

Cynthia A. Cochran

- For the indulgence and support of my friends and pets: thank you!
- To all of my family, who love and inspire me, and especially to all our talented writers, for providing me models to follow: thank you!
- Bob, particularly for your inspiration, useful commentary, and doing the dishes once even though you hated it: thank you!
- Luke Beatty, for inspiring and managing this work – and for all the candy: thank you!

I dedicate my work to my dad, my mom, and my brother Phil.

CONTENTS

ACKNOWLEDGMENTS

Luke and Cindy would like to acknowledge those who helped get this book to the finish line:

- Adam, Emma, Erika, and Garrett, who make Schewe Library the awesome place it is.
- The Illinois College English faculty, for their encouragement.
- Our fabulous editorial team at Routledge: Brian, Nicole, Grant, Tom, and Caroline.
- Our peer-reviewers, who gave us helpful feedback along the way.
- Our impromptu editor, Robert S. Hart, for his helpful suggestions.
- Our basement-dwelling book guru, Jim Streib, for his advice and counsel.
- Colleagues on several listservs (especially WPA and WCenter) who suggested helpful resources.
- The students at Illinois College, whose questions and suggestions were uppermost in our minds as we wrote.
- Janet Monteith, for the germ of an idea.
- Michael Eula, Janet Madden, and James Harner for plowing the field before us.

PREFACE

You're reading this book because you want to write an annotated bibliography. Maybe you've heard of an annotated bibliography before, maybe not. Maybe you've written one before, maybe not. Either way, this book is for you because it will guide you through the process of writing your annotated bibliography from start to finish. We'll tell you what an annotated bibliography is, how to make it, how to polish it, and how to use it in your writing. Whether you're a researcher, undergraduate, graduate student, or high school student, you will succeed in writing your annotated bibliography if you follow our advice.

Who are we and why should you trust us? Luke is a library director and has been working in academic librarianship for over a decade. He's from Canada. Cindy is a writing studies scholar who teaches college writing courses and directs a writing center. She's from the United States. The two of us work at Illinois College, a liberal arts college, and we help students with their research and writing every day.

A few years ago, we noticed that more and more college faculty were assigning annotated bibliographies in their courses. We noticed this because a flood of students continuously sought our help with their assignments. As we spoke with colleagues, we learned that this trend was happening not just on our campus, but on many other campuses as well. In fact, the annotated bibliography is so prolific that it is even being assigned in high school Advance Placement and dual-credit courses.

Why has the annotated bibliography become so popular? In talking with our colleagues, they identified some key reasons. First, the annotated bibliography assignment helps students to carefully select and defend their research. Second, writing an annotated bibliography helps students to take effective shortcuts in the note-taking process. Third, the annotated bibliography feeds nicely into research papers. And fourth, as students advance in their majors, they find it especially helpful when tackling bigger projects.

But there was a problem: nobody had offered a comprehensive resource on writing annotated bibliographies. Students and their instructors could find some help online, but the advice was piecemeal, limited in scope, and in some cases incorrect. Finding high-quality samples of annotated bibliographies was equally difficult. Every resource we found was limited in one way or another. Nobody had created a one-stop annotated bibliography shop – until we wrote this book!

1

SETTING THE STAGE

1.1 Introduction

The annotated bibliography is a common assignment in many courses and a fundamental step in writing research papers. Writing an annotated bibliography for the first time can be daunting, especially because there are so many ways to do it. We hope you use this book as a guide to help you create your annotated bibliography. Here is what you will learn from this book:

- Basic definitions of research terms you need to know
- Format and stylistic conventions of annotated bibliographies
- How to write different annotation types
- What to include (and exclude!) when writing your annotated bibliography
- Good strategies for using annotated bibliographies in your research writing
- Sample annotations and annotated bibliographies in the APA, MLA, and Chicago styles

1.2 Basic Definitions

You will need to know some basic terms and concepts to write your annotated bibliography, and this chapter will introduce you to them. You will also find definitions of bold-faced terms in the Glossary at the end of this book.

1.2.1 What Is a Source?

A **source** is any outside material you use in research and writing. This book focuses mostly on sources that student and other researchers commonly use:

- Books
- Book chapters
- Journal articles
- Magazine articles
- Newspaper articles
- Encyclopedia articles/entries
- Blogs/podcasts
- Websites and webpages
- Videos/films/TV shows
- Government reports/technical reports
- Images/art
- Dissertations

1.2.2 What Is a Citation (aka a Reference)?

A **citation** is a written identifier of a source. Citations typically appear in two places: the body of a research paper and a **bibliography** (a list of sources at the end of a paper to go along with the glossary). Because citations *refer* to sources, they are sometimes called **references**. **In-text citations** (aka internal or parenthetical references) appear in the body of your paper. In some assignments, you may also learn to place citations at the bottom of a page (where they are called **footnotes**), or at the end of the paper (where they are called **endnotes**).

To **cite** a source is to identify its origin. (Never call a citation a "cite." It is wrong and your professor will be most displeased!) Whereas in-text citations may be very brief, citations in bibliographies are much longer, and contain all the **bibliographic information** (i.e., all the identifiers that readers need in order to locate each source, including authors, titles, publisher names, and so on).

There are many **citation styles**, and they correspond to certain fields and professions. In this book we concentrate on the three most popular styles: **American Psychological Association (APA)**, **Modern Language Association (MLA)**, and **Chicago/Turabian** (in this book we use the Chicago Author–Date style, but many also use the Chicago Notes and Bibliography style). Citation styles are also known as **documentation styles**.

1.2.3 What Is a Bibliography?

A bibliography is an organized list of citations, most often presented alphabetically. In APA-style papers, the bibliography is called **References.** In MLA-style papers, the bibliography is called **Works Cited.** In Chicago-style papers, it is called **Bibliography.**

1.2.4 What Is an Annotation?

An **annotation** is a note about a source. To **annotate** is to take notes on a text or artifact. Annotations are generally written in complete sentences, although bulleted lists are sometimes acceptable. Annotations can be very short or very long, depending on your context and needs. Here are the five annotation types:

- **Descriptive annotations** identify the features and main sections of a source
- **Summative annotations** recap the main points and arguments of a source
- **Evaluative annotations** judge the trustworthiness, reliability, and value of a source
- **Reflective annotations** tell where and how one might use a source in one's work
- **Combined annotations** use two to four of the annotation types listed above

1.2.5 What Is an Annotated Bibliography?

An **annotated bibliography** is an organized list of citations in which each citation is annotated. Typically, an annotated bibliography is alphabetized, although it can be arranged in other ways as well (Figure 1.1).

FIGURE 1.1 Sample Annotated Bibliography.
Source: https://is.gd/nZ5GwM. License Attribution: 4.0 International (CC BY 4.0)

1.3 Related Kinds of Writing

You can easily confuse annotated bibliographies with other kinds of writing. Before you invest time in writing an annotated bibliography, make sure you are *not* supposed to be producing one of the following types of writing:

1.3.1 Bibliography

A bibliography, as we have discussed, is an organized list of citations. Bibliographies are found at the end of many research works, including books, chapters, articles, and reports. They also appear in "Further Reading" sections in popular sources, like magazine articles or webpages. People even publish bibliographies – including annotated bibliographies – in standalone form. Bibliographies *do not* contain annotations unless they are annotated bibliographies.

Figure 1.2 shows an example of a published bibliography with several citations (and an introductory note).

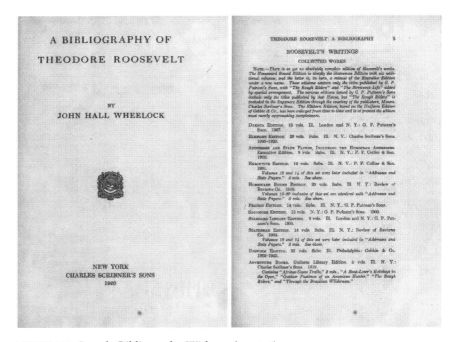

FIGURE 1.2 Sample Bibliography Without Annotations.
Source: https://is.gd/cs7IaQ. Usage Rights: Public Domain

1.3.2 Abstract (aka "Precis," "Synopsis")

An **abstract** is an internationally recognized form of writing (International Organization for Standardization 1976/2019). Typically, an abstract is a one- or two-paragraph summary of a scholarly article, book, or speech that provides readers with a concise overview of the main points and key arguments of a work, including the work's context or purpose; problem or major research questions; methods; findings and analysis; and conclusions. A **precis** is a type of abstract used to summarize a speech or text and is common in business

The state of OA: a large-scale analysis of the prevalence and impact of Open Access articles

Heather Piwowar[1,*], Jason Priem[1,*], Vincent Larivière[2,3], Juan Pablo Alperin[4,5], Lisa Matthias[5], Bree Norlander[6,8], Ashley Farley[2,8], Jevin West[7] and Stefanie Haustein[2,9]

[1] Impactstory, Sanford, NC, USA
[2] École de bibliothéconomie et des sciences de l'information, Université de Montréal, Montréal, QC, Canada
[3] Observatoire des Sciences et des Technologies (OST), Centre Interuniversitaire de Recherche sur la Science et la Technologie (CIRST), Université du Québec à Montréal, Montréal, QC, Canada
[4] Canadian Institute for Studies in Publishing, Simon Fraser University, Vancouver, BC, Canada
[5] Public Knowledge Project, Canada
[6] Scholarly Communications Lab, Simon Fraser University, Vancouver, Canada
[7] Information School, University of Washington, Seattle, USA
[8] FlourishOA, USA
[9] School of Information Studies, University of Ottawa, Ottawa, ON, Canada
[*] These authors contributed equally to this work.

Submitted 9 August 2017
Accepted 25 January 2018
Published 13 February 2018

Corresponding authors
Heather Piwowar,
heather@impactstory.org
Jason Priem, jason@impactstory.org

Academic editor
Robert McDonald

Additional Information and Declarations can be found on page 19

DOI 10.7717/peerj.4375

ABSTRACT

Despite growing interest in Open Access (OA) to scholarly literature, there is an unmet need for large-scale, up-to-date, and reproducible studies assessing the prevalence and characteristics of OA. We address this need using oaDOI, an open online service that determines OA status for 67 million articles. We use three samples, each of 100,000 articles, to investigate OA in three populations: (1) all journal articles assigned a Crossref DOI, (2) recent journal articles indexed in Web of Science, and (3) articles viewed by users of Unpaywall, an open-source browser extension that lets users find OA articles using oaDOI. We estimate that at least 28% of the scholarly literature is OA (19M in total) and that this proportion is growing, driven particularly by growth in Gold and Hybrid. The most recent year analyzed (2015) also has the highest percentage of OA (45%). Because of this growth, and the fact that readers disproportionately access newer articles, we find that Unpaywall users encounter OA quite frequently: 47% of articles they view are OA. Notably, the most common mechanism for OA is not Gold, Green, or Hybrid OA, but rather an under-discussed category we dub Bronze: articles made free-to-read on the publisher website, without an explicit Open license. We also examine the citation impact of OA articles, corroborating the so-called open-access citation advantage: accounting for age and discipline, OA articles receive 18% more citations than average, an effect driven primarily by Green and Hybrid OA. We encourage further research using the free oaDOI service, as a way to inform OA policy and practice.

Subjects Legal Issues, Science Policy, Data Science
Keywords Open access, Open science, Scientometrics, Publishing, Libraries, Scholarly communication, Bibliometrics, Science policy

How to cite this article Piwowar et al. (2018), The state of OA: a large-scale analysis of the prevalence and impact of Open Access articles. PeerJ 6:e4375; DOI 10.7717/peerj.4375

FIGURE 1.3 Sample Abstract.

Source: https://is.gd/bIJD5h. License Attribution: 4.0 International (CC BY 4.0)

writing. A **synopsis** is a type of abstract as well, but typically refers to summaries of artistic works.

An abstract normally appears immediately before the introduction of a scholarly article, book, or conference paper. Abstracts are also found in library databases, conference proceedings, and tables of contents.

Though an abstract and a summative annotation may seem quite similar, an abstract is written from an objective perspective (on the key points of a source), whereas a summative annotation is written from your viewpoint (on what you find most important). The abstract, by addressing only one source, also differs from annotated bibliographies, which have entries for many sources (Figure 1.3).

1.3.3 Book Review

As implied by the name, a **book review** applies only to books! Book reviews can be short (sometimes a paragraph or two) or quite long (we have seen 20-page book reviews). The book review gives the reader a sense of what the book is about and a condensed version of what the book says. Most book reviews critique a book's content or ideas. Sometimes you can find a review of several related books, but most reviews are about only one. As a genre, book reviews are prominent in newspapers, magazines, academic journals, and a variety of online sites (Amazon.com, Reddit, book clubs, etc.).

Unlike annotated bibliographies, book reviews do not necessarily follow a set structure, nor do they usually contain bibliographic citations (Figure 1.4).

1.3.4 Research Paper

A **research paper** is an essay in which a writer uses various sources to support a thesis. The research paper contains a bibliography of all the sources cited in the paper.

The research paper is assigned in high school, undergraduate, and graduate classes of all kinds, not only writing courses. At the graduate and professional levels, a research paper typically takes the form of a book, scholarly article, thesis, or dissertation.

Unlike an annotated bibliography, which is in list form, the research paper is a narrative, and maybe an argument. Though annotated bibliographies can be integral to preparing a research paper, students should complete the annotated bibliography before sitting down to compose their paper. In this way, writing the annotated bibliography becomes a useful part of the research-writing process (Figure 1.5).

European Review of Latin American and Caribbean Studies
Revista Europea de Estudios Latinoamericanos y del Caribe

107 (2019): January-June, book review 5
www.erlacs.org

Book Review

– *Mortal Doubt: Transnational Gangs and Social Order in Guatemala City*, by
Anthony W. Fontes. University of California Press, 2018.

In this critical, well-researched, and well-written study, Anthony W. Fontes
uses extensive ethnographic research in Guatemala City to argue that
Guatemala's postwar social order is affected by the symbolic rendering of
maras (transnational gangs). Fontes explains the importance of seeing past the
charades and spectacles of transnational gangs to bring into visibility how
"regimes of rumour" (p. 17) enmeshed with tangible acts of crime in postwar
Guatemala turn transnational gangs into "a key site upon which competing
projects to control, order, and dominate Guatemalan society are exposed in all
their violent contradiction" (p. 14). Rather than assuming that transnational
gangs are the only problem worth researching in Guatemala City, Fontes forces
the reader, through a compilation of interviews with former gang members,
members of gang rehabilitation programs, family members of gang members,
journalists, etc. to challenge this assumption and instead investigate how the
symbolic and the material give shape to ways of constructing/understanding
the gang phenomenon and establishing a social order in time of uncertainty.

Fontes's book sheds light on two key areas that enrich gang literature: (1)
awareness on engaging ethnographically with the material and imagined role of
a *marero* (gangster), constructed and reproduced by both *marero* and society at
large. The interplay between truth and rumour that informs the confusing and
mortal social order. And (2) challenging the popular image of the *marero* as
being inherently deviant and thus different from other humans. This awareness
is also crucial to incorporate in studies because it can then challenge the
dominant local and transnational symbolic image of gangs as irrationally
violent groups who appear and exist as mere outcomes of civil wars and
economic disparity. The author's ethnographical engagement with the material
and imagined role of *marero* throughout the book substantiates his analysis.

Fontes recognizes while observing and analyzing his data that the symbolic
and material forms of knowledge produce a sort of truth accepted by those who
repeat that particular narrative. Fontes's ability to identify moments in which
his informants are spewing fantasies to enrich their narratives, when they are

DOI: http://doi.org/10.32992/erlacs.10478 © Vanesa Tomasino Rodriguez. Open Access book
review distributed under the terms of the Creative Commons Attribution 4.0 Unported (CC BY
4.0) License https://creativecommons.org/licenses/by/4.0/.

WWW.ERLACS.ORG is published by CEDLA – Centre for Latin American Research and
Documentation | Centro de Estudios y Documentación Latinoamericanos, Amsterdam; The
Netherlands | Países Bajos; www.cedla.uva.nl; ISSN 0924-0608, eISSN 1879-4750.

FIGURE 1.4   Sample Book Review.

Source: https://is.gd/4RlNzn. License Attribution: 4.0 International (CC BY 4.0)

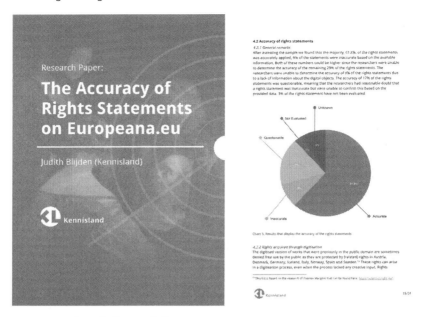

FIGURE 1.5 Sample Research Paper.
Source: https://is.gd/BYn5Ak. License Attribution: 4.0 International (CC BY 4.0)

1.3.5 Literature Review

A **literature review** is a narrative that summarizes, evaluates, and synthesizes the scholarship on a given topic. The purpose of a literature review is to provide an informative and pointed context for research. Most literature reviews include only the most important and relevant scholarship. On the other hand, a **comprehensive literature review** includes *all* the relevant scholarship on a given topic. A **systematic literature review** discusses the relevant scholarship in a highly methodical manner. Most literature reviews of any kind critically appraise the scholarship under consideration.

Literature reviews are normally part of larger scholarly works. They appear in journal articles and research proposals, typically following an introductory section. A literature review in a book or dissertation is typically its own chapter, and is typically more comprehensive than a literature review in an article.

Unlike an annotated bibliography, a literature review is a narrative. In other words, it tells the research story of a topic. An annotated bibliography, however, contains only parts of a research story and is a list (Figure 1.6).

Literature Review - Original Research

A Systematic Literature Review on Professional Identity Construction in Social Media

SAGE Open
January-March 2019: 1–11
© The Author(s) 2019
DOI: 10.1177/2158244019828847
journals.sagepub.com/home/sgo
SAGE

Judita Kasperiuniene[1] and Vilma Zydziunaite[1]

Abstract

The aim of this systematic review was to gather, review, summarize, and analyze the studies on professional identity construction in social media from various scholar perspectives. The search was conducted on the WoS Core Collection, Scopus, and EBSCOhost databases using keywords "professional identity construction" and "social media." Seventeen full-text articles were studied searching for the essential aspects of professional identity construction. Results discussed professional identity as a complex phenomenon with two dominating perspectives: (a) professional identity as a cognitive structure and (b) professional identity as a social construct. Cognitive structures of professional identity construction in social media were mainly or partially covered in education, communication, and medical tourism-related contexts. Studies that envisage professional identity as socially constructed dominate in management, organizational, medical tourism, and neuroscience. The core topics of professional identity construction cover the blurring of professional stereotypes and reconstruction of multiple professional selves; merging public and private identities; belonging to a group and trusting social media. In researched papers, scholars argue virtual behavior can be predicted and smart technologies could help maintain physical and psychological balance. Findings show the overlapping landscape of studies and identify areas for future interdisciplinary research.

Keywords

identity construction, professional self-presentation, systematic literature review, social media

Introduction

Professional identity is described as a homogeneous whole of the professional and personal self and can be studied from two perspectives. Researchers representing the first perspective investigated how an individual, as a part of a social structure, could influence identity construction. The other perspective deals with how the person as a group leader could influence the development of social structures. Almost 20 years ago, Stryker and Burke (2000) raised challenges that remain unresolved: how these two perspectives of *identity theory* are linked. In this article, we connect both perspectives, taking into consideration that they are equally important in understanding the professional self, interactions, and structures.

Although the notion of *professional* identity is the most widespread, some scholars speak about *vocational* identity (X. Li, Hou, & Jia, 2015) or *career* identity (Lysova, Richardson, Khapova, & Jansen, 2015) by identifying them with professional identity and using these three different terms alternatively. *Professional identity* has been extensively studied by scholars in social science, medicine,

business and management, communication and information sciences. Multiple dimensions of identity, such as race, culture, class, religion, gender, or sexual orientation are explained and empirically grounded (Jones & McEwen, 2000). The professional roles of employees in different professions as a part of professional identity are empirically tested. For example, Akkerman and Meijer (2011) elaborated a professional identity as (a) simultaneously unitary and multiple, (b) continuous and discontinuous, and (c) individual and the same time social. Authors revealed that the coherent and consistent sense of a professional self within the professional identity could be maintained through a variety of individual and group participation and self-investment throughout the professional career (Akkerman & Meijer, 2011). In their qualitative longitudinal study on professional

[1]Vytautas Magnus University, Kaunas, Lithuania

Corresponding Author:
Judita Kasperiuniene, Vytautas Magnus University, Jonavos g. 66, 44191 Kaunas, Lithuania.
Email: judita.kasperiuniene@vdu.lt

FIGURE 1.6 Sample Literature Review.

Source: https://is.gd/lpKz9b. License Attribution: 4.0 International (CC BY 4.0)

1.3.6 Bibliographic Essay

A **bibliographic essay** is a special form of a literature review. Like a literature review, it summarizes relevant research; like an annotated bibliography, it includes entries with bibliographic information. Unlike an annotated bibliography,

FIGURE 1.7 Sample Bibliographic Essay.

Source: https://is.gd/zIWkdn. License Attribution: 4.0 International (CC BY 4.0)

however, it is not a list, but rather a narrative. In a way, the bibliographic essay is an annotated bibliography in narrative form.

Like the annotated bibliography, bibliographic essays are published in scholarly books and academic journals, as well as in various online forums (e.g., scholarly societies, academic blogs, etc.). Also, like the annotated bibliography, the bibliographic essay prepares people to do further research in a given area (Figure 1.7).

1.4 How to Use This Book

This book is divided into chapters that each deal with a different aspect of the annotated bibliography.

Chapter 2: Citation and Documentation Styles

If you are new to the research writing process, begin with *Chapter 2: Citation and Documentation Styles*, which defines citations, explains why citations matter, and tells the story of why different documentation styles exist. It then presents a comparison chart of the leading citation styles (i.e., APA, MLA, Chicago).

Chapter 3: The Format and Look of the Annotated Bibliography

In *Chapter 3: The Format and Look of the Annotated Bibliography*, you will learn how to summarize, paraphrase, and occasionally quote in your annotations. You will also learn common formatting and style considerations. This part also tells you how to judge the depth to which your annotation should go.

Chapter 4: Types of Annotations

Chapter 4: Types of Annotations explains the descriptive, summative, evaluative, reflective, and combined annotation types. The chapter includes checklists to use while writing your annotated bibliography.

Chapter 5: Annotating Different Kinds of Sources

Go to *Chapter 5: Annotating Different Kinds of Sources* to learn about annotating various kinds of sources (e.g., book chapters, academic articles, blogs, etc.). You will find plenty of tips and examples for each kind of source.

Chapter 6: Composing Your Annotations

Once you have written your annotated bibliography and you are about to write your research paper, go to *Chapter 6: Composing Your Annotations*, which will help you take notes efficiently no matter what kinds of sources you have.

Chapter 7: Crunch Time – Annotated Bibliography in Process

Chapter 7: Crunch Time – Annotated Bibliography in Process is useful because it teaches you to use your annotated bibliography to ease into writing your research paper. You will learn to transform your annotated bibliography into a References/Works Cited/Bibliography, a workspace for notes, an outline, and even a rough draft of your research paper.

Chapter 8: Tools and Strategies for Working Online

Chapter 8: Tools and Strategies for Working Online describes the use of online citation and bibliographic tools to help you with your work. It also explains good ways to write annotated bibliographies when you are working in a group in an online context. Finally, it discusses how to use online platforms when you want to publish or share your annotated bibliography.

Chapter 9: Sample Annotated Bibliographies

Upper-level and graduate students will find good advice and plenty of examples in *Chapter 9: Sample Annotated Bibliographies*. There you will find three sample annotated bibliographies in the APA, MLA, and Chicago styles.

1.5 Further Reading

We introduced several concepts in this chapter, and if you would like to know more about them, we suggest you have a look at the following:

1.5.1 Annotations

Burkle-Young, Francis A., and Saundra Maley. *The Art of the Footnote[1]: The Intelligent Student's Guide to the Art and Science of Annotating Texts.* University Press of America, 1996.

Hauptman, Robert. *Documentation: A History and Critique of Attribution, Commentary, Glosses, Marginalia, Notes, Bibliographies, Works-cited Lists, and Citation Indexing and Analysis.* McFarland, 2008.

Zerby, Chuck. *The Devil's Details: A History of Footnotes.* Simon & Schuster, 2003.

1.5.2 Bibliographies

Harmon, Robert B. *Elements of Bibliography: A Guide to Information Sources and Practical Applications.* 3rd ed., Scarecrow Press, 1998.

Krummel, Donald William. *Bibliographies, Their Aims and Methods.* H.W. Wilson Co., 1984.

Robinson, Anthony Meredith Lewis, and Margaret Lodder. *Systematic Bibliography: A Practical Guide to the Work of Compilation.* 4th ed., C. Bingley, 1979.

1.5.3 Book Reviews

Calvani, Mayra, and Anne K. Edwards. *The Slippery Art of Book Reviewing.* Twilight Times Books, 2008.

Hyland, Ken, and Giuliana Diani. *Academic Evaluation: Review Genres in University Settings.* Palgrave Macmillan, 2009.

Pool, Gail. *Faint Praise: The Plight of Book Reviewing in America.* University of Missouri Press, 2007.

1.5.4 Literature Reviews

Booth, Andrew, et al. *Systematic Approaches to a Successful Literature Review.* 2nd ed., Sage, 2016.

Efron, Sara Efrat, and Ruth Ravid. *Writing the Literature Review: A Practical Guide*. The Guilford Press, 2019.

Jesson, Jill, et al. *Doing Your Literature Review: Traditional and Systematic Techniques*. Sage, 2011.

1.5.5 Research Papers

Lester, James D., and James D. Lester Jr. *Writing Research Papers: A Complete Guide*. 15th ed., Pearson, 2018.

Winkler, Anthony C., and Jo Ray McCuen. *Writing the Research Paper: A Handbook*. 8th ed., Thomson Wadsworth, 2012.

1.5.6 Sources

Harvey, Gordon. *Writing with Sources: A Guide for Students*. 3rd ed., Hackett Publishing Company, Inc., 2017.

Spatt, Brenda. *Writing from Sources*. 9th ed., Bedford/St. Martin's, 2016.

Wallraff, Barbara. *Your Own Words*. Counterpoint, 2004.

Works Cited

International Organization for Standardization. "ISO 214:1976(En), Documentation — Abstracts for Publications and Documentation." *ISO Online Browsing Platform (OBP)*, www.iso.org/obp/ui/#iso:std:iso:214:ed-1:v1:en

2

CITATION AND DOCUMENTATION STYLES

2.1 Citation Styles

You have your annotated bibliography assignment – now what? Though this book is not a citation manual *per se*, you can quickly read this chapter to review the basic features of a citation and documentation styles. This chapter covers the most important citation issues and explains why different documentation styles exist for different fields of study. Specifically, we cover the American Psychological Association (APA), Modern Language Association (MLA), and Chicago styles in this chapter. If you are already comfortable citing material, feel free to jump ahead to *Chapter 3: The Format and Look of the Annotated Bibliography*.

2.1.1 Basics of Citations

Citations (aka references) appear in research writing in the text, footnotes, or endnotes. They also appear in the References/Bibliography/Works Cited list, and of course the annotated bibliography itself. Citations identify the bibliographic information of your sources in a format that conveys this information quickly and efficiently. The exact format of a citation depends upon the kind of source being described, as well as the documentation style being used (e.g., APA, MLA, Chicago, or any other).

By listing citations in an annotated bibliography, you provide an easy way for your readers to find and access your sources. That is because the citations specify author(s), title(s), date(s) of publication, and other pertinent information as needed (e.g., page numbers, name of a work's editor or translator, publisher, database(s) where you found your source, etc.).

2.1.2 Why Cite Sources?

Putting citations in your annotated bibliography is especially important to you and your readers because that way you give credit to the original authors and you avoid plagiarism. However, there are six additional reasons to cite sources in your annotated bibliography:

- You have a record that makes it easy for you to gain access to your sources later
- You can keep your resources straight so that you can correctly cite the sources you end up using in your paper
- You can demonstrate the extent of your hard research work to your instructor
- Your instructor can check your list of sources to ensure you are consulting high-quality and course-appropriate material
- Your instructor or librarian can use your citations to help you fill any gaps you may have in your research
- You can re-use the citations from your annotated bibliography when you later need to create a References/Bibliography/Works Cited list or outline

If you publish an annotated bibliography, your citations may also help other researchers. They may have various motivations to consult your citations. By scanning your citations, readers can quickly ascertain the nature and scope of your topic, which can help them identify sources for their own research.

2.1.3 What Are Citation/Documentation Styles?

There are many different formats for citing sources, each one used in certain professions and regions of the world. These are called citation styles or documentation styles. You are most likely going to need to learn at least one of the three most popular documentation styles in use in the United States: APA, MLA, and Chicago. Other formats include the following:

- ACS style, used by the American Chemical Society
- AMA style, used by the American Medical Association
- ASA style, used by the American Sociological Association
- Bluebook, the most frequently used citation style in legal writing
- CSE style, used by the Council of Science Editors
- Harvard style, an author–date citation system used by researchers at many British and Commonwealth universities
- IEEE style, used by the Institute of Electrical and Electronics Engineers, commonly used in engineering and computer science

- Linguistics Style Sheet, used by the Linguistics Society of America
- MHRA style, the Modern Humanities Research Association format, used in British humanities journals
- Oxford style, commonly used in Australia as well as at Oxford and other United Kingdom universities
- Oxford Standard Citation of Legal Authorities (OSCOLA), used in legal writing, especially in Australia and the United Kingdom
- Turabian, used as a student-friendly variant of the Chicago style of documenting sources

2.1.4 Why Different Styles? A Brief History

The answer is both historical and logical. Without getting into the thorny details, citation formats emerged historically as a way for people around the world to exchange information about items owned in private collections, church libraries, and university libraries. Bibliographies themselves date back to the second century when a physician named Galen published an organized list

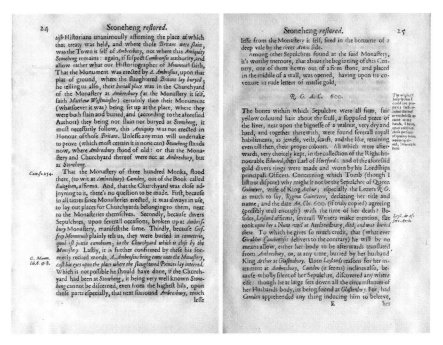

FIGURE 2.1 Sample of Pre-1800 Annotation.

Source: https://is.gd/x8HJQ9. License Attribution: Public Domain of his own works in which he also denounced works falsely attributed to him (Balsamo 7). Early on, the Catholic Church created lists of religious scholarship, as did holders of other libraries. The annotated bibliography emerged as a way to tell people about the resources in these libraries.

Annotations and citations before the 1600s were erratic because they were left to the whims of whoever compiled them. They could appear at the top, side, or bottom of a page, for example. By the 17th century, citations were still not perfectly consistent, but by that time scholars tended to use "complex full-cite, letter-and-number systems that used Latin terms" (Connors 11). Whereas earlier citations tended to be placed, along with remarks, in the margins of the text, by the 1700s many scholars now placed citations and annotations in footnotes (32). Connors, in writing about the persuasive power of citation systems, credits Edward Gibbon's 1776 *The History of the Decline and Fall of the Roman Empire* (1776–1787) as the first volume in which citations became a consistent "literary form" (35). The citations included author, title, volume, place of publication, and section or page (36) (Figure 2.1).

FIGURE 2.2 Sample of Pre-1800 Annotation and Citation.
Source: https://is.gd/gO83lp. License Attribution: Public Domain

Before the 1800s, most scholarship had a generally educated audience, but by the 1900s, the professions grew and scholars became more narrowly focused (Connors 39, 42). Many scholars, publishers, and editors saw the need to systemize the format of citations for various kinds of sources, and thus, citations became standardized. However, different citation systems evolved in response to the varied needs of professionals, the kinds of sources they used, and the reasons they used the sources (Figure 2.2).

Several citation systems emerged in the 19th and 20th centuries. For example, the US Geological Service and the US Government Printing Office developed their own style guides in the 1890s (Connors 43). The Harvard style was developed at Harvard University by Edward Laurens Mark, and was probably modeled on the Library of Harvard's Museum of Comparative Zoology system for cataloging museum artifacts (Chernin 1062–1063). However, there were still a variety of citation and annotation styles, that were inconsistent with one another (Figure 2.3).

To date, hundreds of documentation styles are in use throughout the world. They vary tremendously, and students have resented those variations since the beginning of documented scholarship!

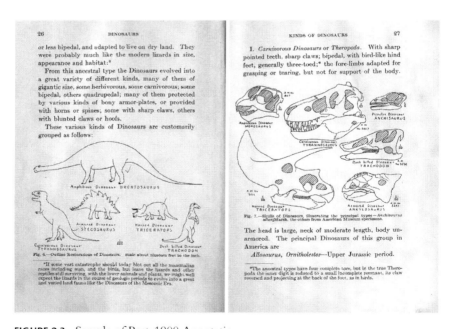

FIGURE 2.3 Sample of Post-1900 Annotation.
Source: https://is.gd/Ir8sMa. License Attribution: Public Domain

2.2 Main Documentation Styles

The three most common documentation styles are APA, MLA, and Chicago. Although citations in these styles have many similarities, the differences between the styles matter. Below, you will find the basic elements for citing a book and a journal article in the APA, MLA, and Chicago styles.

2.2.1 APA

The APA was first produced in 1929, and is commonly used by researchers in the social sciences, especially psychology, education, sociology, and sometimes writing studies. This style is also used in the natural and physical sciences and some classes at the undergraduate level.

Elements in a citation include items such as author names and the titles of articles and books. However, not every element is used in every citation (that depends on the kind of source you are citing and the documentation style you are using).

The most essential elements in an APA citation include the following:

- Creator and other contributors (initials for given names)
- Year
- Title(s)
- Version, volume, and issue number, if any
- Location of publisher (omitted in the seventh edition)
- Publisher
- Publication date
- Page numbers used
- Virtual location, if used (URL or Digital Object Identifier [DOI], database if no URL or DOI)

Here is a basic format for citing a book in APA style:

> Author Last Name, First Initial. Middle Initial. (Year of publication). *Title of work: Capital letter also for subtitle's first word.* Location: Publisher.

Here is the basic format for citing a *book* in APA and an example citation:

Author Last Name, First Initial. Second Initial. (Year). *Title of book: Subtitle of book.* Location: Publisher.
Babcock, R. D., & Daniels, S. (2017). *Writing centers and disability.* Southlake, Texas: Fountainhead Press.

Here is the basic format for citing a *journal article* in APA and an example citation:

> Author Last Name, First Initial. Second Initial. (Year). Article title: Article subtitle. *Journal Title Capitalized, volume number* (issue number), pages, URL or DOI if available.

> Cochran, P. (2015). Big fish stories: Analysis of historical newspaper data on size of lake sturgeon (*Acipenser fulvescens*) in the Lake Michigan Basin. *Michigan Academician, 42*(1), 26–39.

For other examples, see the APA's *Publication Manual of the American Psychological Association*.

2.2.2 MLA

The MLA style is popular in the humanities, especially English, art history, language, linguistics, music, religion, and philosophy. In the United States, students learn this style in high school or in their first year of college, and it is sometimes used in undergraduate social science, business, and science courses.

The MLA first released its system in 1951 as "The MLA Style Sheet." This was replaced in 1977 by the *MLA Handbook for Writers of Research Papers, Theses, and Dissertations,* which was subsequently retitled *MLA Handbook for Writers of Research Papers* in 2003, and now is simply the *MLA Handbook* (various editions).

Here are the most important elements in an MLA citation (but remember to omit elements that do not pertain to a given source):

- Creators and other contributors, if any (full names)
- Title of source and its container(s)
- Version, volume and issue numbers, if any
- City of publication (may be omitted)
- Publisher
- Publication date
- Database name, if any
- Virtual location, if used (URL or DOI)

Here are how these elements appear in an MLA citation:

> Author. Title. Title of container (normally self-contained if book), Other contributors (translators or editors), Version (edition), Number (vol. and/or no.), Publisher, Publication Date, Location (pp.). Second container's title, Other contributors, Version, Number, Publisher, Publication date, Location (page range if only a part of the container is used).

Here is the basic format for citing a *book* in MLA and an example citation:

Author Last Name, First Name Second Initial. *Title of Book: Subtitle of Book.* Publisher, year.
Cochran, Randy. *Critter Golf: The Adventures at Owl's Nest.* Outskirts Press, 2013.

Here is the basic format for citing a *journal article* in MLA and an example citation:

Author Last Name, First Initial. Second Initial. (Year). Article title. *Journal Title.* Volume number, Issue number (Date published): page range. For online sources, DOI or URL if available.
Spiro, Rand J., et al. "Cognitive Flexibility, Constructivism, and Hypertext: Random Access Instruction for Advanced Knowledge Acquisition in Ill-Structured Domains." Educational Technology, vol. 31, no. 5, 1991, pp. 24–33.

For other examples, see a resource such as the *MLA Handbook.*

2.2.3 Chicago Style

The Chicago style is often used in history, philosophy, religion, and art history. *The Chicago Manual of Style* has been used since it was first published in 1906 by the University of Chicago Press.

Here are the most essential elements in a Chicago style citation (but remember to omit elements that do not pertain to a given source):

- Creators and other contributor(s) (full names)
- Title of source and its container(s)
- Version, volume and issue numbers, if any
- City of publication
- Publisher
- Publication date
- Virtual location (database, URL, or DOI)

Here is a basic format for citing a book in the Chicago Style:

Last name, First name Middle initial. *Title of Book: Subtitle of Book.* Place of Publication: Publisher, year.

Here is the basic format for citing a *book* in Chicago and an example citation:

Last name, First name Middle name or initial. *Title of Book: Subtitle of Book.* Place of Publication: Publisher, year.
Enos, Richard Leo. *Greek Rhetoric before Aristotle.* 2nd ed. Anderson, S.C: Parlor Press, 2011.

Here is the basic format for citing a *journal article* in Chicago and an example citation:

Author Last Name, First Name. "Article Title." *Journal Name* Volume Number, Issue Number (Year): Page Range. For online sources, Accessed: access date. URL or DOI.
Cochran, Jessica. "Let's Do It! The Center for Book and Paper Arts: A History." *The Journal of Artists' Books* no. 46, Fall (2019): 3–13.

For more examples, see *The Chicago Manual of Style.*

2.3 Important Features of MLA, APA, and Chicago Styles

Some of the most important distinguishing features of APA, MLA, and Chicago documentation styles, including formatting considerations, can be found in Table 2.1.

2.4 Further Reading

We introduced several concepts in this chapter, and if you would like to know more about them, we suggest you have a look at the following:

2.4.1 APA Citation and Documentation Style

American Psychological Association. "APA Style Blog." *APA Style Blog,* 2019, https://is.gd/CVuhnf

American Psychological Association. *Publication Manual of the American Psychological Association.* 6th ed., American Psychological Association, 2010.

2.4.2 MLA Citation and Documentation Style

Modern Language Association of America. *MLA Handbook.* 8th ed., Modern Language Association of America, 2016.

Modern Language Association of America. *MLA Style Manual and Guide to Scholarly Publishing*. 3rd ed., Modern Language Association of America, 2008.
Modern Language Association of America. "Works Cited: A Quick Guide." *The MLA Style Center*, 2019, https://is.gd/OIRn67

TABLE 2.1 Comparison Chart of Leading Documentation Styles

Feature	APA	MLA	Chicago
Who most commonly uses this style?	Natural, social, and physical sciences	Arts and humanities	History, religion, and philosophy
Title of the references list in a research paper, centered on first line of last page of paper	References	Works Cited	Bibliography or References
Pagination/ Running Head	Title, writer's surname, page numbers at top of page	Writer's last name and page numbers ½ inch from top of page, starting on the second page	Page numbers and writer's surname (optional) starting on the second page
Annotated bibliography title, centered on first line of the page	Annotated Bibliography (may contain a subtitle after a colon)	Annotated Bibliography (may contain a subtitle after a colon)	Annotated Bibliography (may contain a subtitle after a colon)
In-text citations (in parentheses)	(Author, year) or (Author, year, page) e.g., (Jones, 2019) or (Jones, 2019, p. 33)	(Author page), e.g., (Jones 33)	(Author date) or (Author date, page) e.g., (Jones 2019) or (Jones 2019, 33)
Example format of referenced authors' names in citations in the bibliographic list	Smith, A. S. or Smith, A. S., & Bourbon, L. L.	Smith, Andrea S. or Smith, Andrea S., and Leo L. Bourbon	Smith, Andrea S. or Smith, Andrea S. and Leo L. Bourbon
Order of list is usually alphabetical	Alphabetized by author, then chronological from earliest to most recent for authors with multiple works	Alphabetized by author, then alphabetical by title of works for authors with multiple works	Alphabetized by author, then alphabetized by title of work for authors with multiple works

2.4.3 Chicago Citation and Documentation Style

The University of Chicago Press. "Chicago-Style Citation: A Quick Guide." *The Chicago Manual of Style Online*, 2017, https://is.gd/uNmKlS
The University of Chicago Press, editor. *The Chicago Manual of Style*. 17th ed., The University of Chicago Press 2017b.

2.4.4 Other Academic Styles

American Medical Association, editor. *AMA Manual of Style: A Guide for Authors and Editors*. 11th ed., Oxford University Press, 2020.
American Sociological Association, editor. *American Sociological Association Style Guide*. 6th ed., American Sociological Association 2019.
Coghill, Anne M., and Lorrin R. Garson, editors. *The ACS Style Guide: Effective Communication of Scientific Information*. 3rd ed., Oxford University Press, 2006.
Columbia Law Review, et al., editors. *The Bluebook: A Uniform System of Citation*. 20th ed., The Harvard Law Review Association, 2015.
Council of Science Editors, editors. *Scientific Style and Format: The CSE Manual for Authors, Editors, and Publishers*. 8th ed., University of Chicago Press, 2014.
Kmiec, David, and Bernadette Longo. *The IEEE Guide to Writing in the Engineering and Technical Fields*. John Wiley and Sons, Inc, 2017.
Oxford University Press, editor. *New Oxford Style Manual*. 3rd ed., Oxford University Press 2016.
Turabian, Kate L. *A Manual for Writers of Research Papers, Theses, and Dissertations: Chicago Style for Students and Researchers*. Edited by Wayne C. Booth et al., 9th ed., University of Chicago Press, 2018.

Works Cited

Balsamo, Luigi. *Bibliography: History of a Tradition*. B.M. Rosenthal, 1990.
Chernin, Eli. "The 'Harvard System': A Mystery Dispelled." *British Medical Journal*, vol. 297, no. 6655, Oct. 1988, pp. 1062–1063, doi:10.1136/bmj.297.6655.1062.
Connors, Robert J. "The Rhetoric of Citation Systems, Part I: The Development of Annotation Structures from the Renaissance to 1900." *Rhetoric Review*, vol. 17, no. 1, 1998, pp. 6–48.

3

THE FORMAT AND LOOK OF THE ANNOTATED BIBLIOGRAPHY

As you prepare to write your annotated bibliography, first set yourself up for success by creating a note-taking plan and familiarizing yourself with some crucial rules. Specifically, you should have a good understanding of how to format your annotated bibliography, and you should also know how to paraphrase and quote a source. This chapter explains how to set up a writing plan; describes the overall format of an annotated bibliography (including its pagination, headers, footers, and title); and lists common stylistic conventions (first-person pronouns, paraphrases, and quotations in your annotations).

3.1 Aim for Success: Set up Your Plan

Once you have a topic for your research, your first step to success is to make a plan. When planning your research, set aside enough time to read, take notes, annotate, write, and revise your work as necessary. If you do this, you will find that the annotated bibliography will save you a huge amount of time in your research-writing process.

Starting early is crucial! Until learning and practicing the research process, many students find out too late that they have not started early enough. They have not allowed themselves enough time to create a good annotated bibliography prior to writing their research paper. Even when the final paper is a research proposal, the annotated bibliography must be complete before the proposal is very far under way. For longer works, such as term papers, senior capstone projects, master's theses, and doctoral dissertations, writing the annotated bibliography is a crucial step.

You can use a simple plan for creating an annotated bibliography in only three stages:

1. Set up your document format
2. Add your citations (in alphabetical order)
3. Add the annotations

3.2 Page Format of the Annotated Bibliography

Annotated bibliographies follow a set format, as you will see in the examples below. The annotated bibliography has a title, *may* include **prefatory matter**, lists citations, and includes annotations (each annotation immediately following its respective citation). In some annotated bibliographies, the annotation begins immediately after the citation (on the same line), but we prefer the format where the annotation paragraph begins on a new line (with a space between the citation and the annotation). In the preferred version (Figure 3.1), the annotation should line up with the indented part of the citation. In the less preferred version (Figure 3.2), the annotation should begin flush left. (For details on creating a Modern Language Association (MLA)-style annotated bibliography for publication, see *Chapter 8: Tools and Strategies for Working Online.*)

[Header starting on page 2]

Allen Mostel
Prof. Lucasz Lockwood
Course #
Date

Annotated Bibliography: My Topic

Prefatory remarks with thesis, followed by sources entries and annotations. Entries are alphabetically organized by author's last name.

Anagram, Annie. *An Extremely Long Book About Extremely Important Things: A Treatise.* Scholarly Publishing, Inc., 2019.

> The first source annotation paragraph follows immediately after the first source's citation. The paragraph is flush left in line with the indented part of the citation, and the paragraph has as many sentences as you need. Most annotations are one paragraph long, but an annotation can contain as many paragraphs as you need. Put an extra space after this paragraph and before the next citation.

Blogger, Bob. *Boring Things You Will Never Need to Know: Burgers & Their Makers.* Bedford/St. Martin's Press, 2017.

> The second source annotation paragraph follows immediately after the second source's citation. Again, the paragraph is flush left in line with the indented part of the citation, and the paragraph has as many sentences as you need. Most annotations are one paragraph long, but they can be as many paragraphs as you need.

Clogger, Carla. *Fifty Methods of Catching Rattle Snakes: A Manual for Beginners.* Prentice Hall, 2019.

> The third source annotation paragraph follows immediately after the third source's citation. The paragraph is flush left in line with the indented part of the citation.

> If you add a second paragraph, make it indented in the same way as the other paragraph in your annotation.

Figure 3.1 Preferred Format for an MLA Annotated Bibliography Page.

[Header starting on page 2]

Allen Mostel
Prof. Lucasz Lockwood
Course #
Date

Annotated Bibliography: My Topic

Prefatory remarks with thesis, followed by sources entries and annotations. Entries are alphabetically organized by author's last name.

Anagram, Annie. *An Extremely Long Book About Extremely Important Things: A Treatise.*
Scholarly Publishing, Inc., 2019.

The first source annotation paragraph follows immediately after the first source's citation. The paragraph is flush left, and the paragraph has as many sentences as you need. Most annotations are one paragraph long, but an annotation can contain as many paragraphs as you need. Put an extra space after this paragraph and before the next citation.

Blogger, Bob. *Boring Things You Will Never Need to Know: Burgers & Their Makers.*
Bedford/St. Martin's Press, 2017.

The second source annotation paragraph follows immediately after the second source's citation. Again, the paragraph is flush left, and the annotation has as many sentences as you need. Most annotations are one paragraph long, but they can be as many paragraphs as you need.

Clogger, Carla. *Fifty Methods of Catching Rattle Snakes: A Manual for Beginners.*
Prentice Hall, 2019.

The third source annotation paragraph follows immediately after the third source's citation. The paragraph is flush left.

If you add a second paragraph, make it indented in the same way as the other paragraph in your annotation.

Figure 3.2 Alternative Format for an MLA Annotated Bibliography Page.

3.2.1 Create Your Page Margins

Choose a margin. Most annotated bibliography formats require margins to be set at 1 inch or 1.5 inches from the edge of the page, but check your documentation guide or your instructor's requirements. Usually you can use the default margin in Microsoft Word, Google Docs, and other word processors.

3.2.2 Pagination, Header, and Footer

Use page numbers in the header, typically starting on the second page. Your documentation style or instructor may have further requirements. For example, if using MLA style, place the header in the upper right-hand corner of each page, starting on the second page, and set the header a half-inch from the top of the page. The header should have your surname and page number. If using American Psychological Association (APA), the title should be flush left and the page number flush right, a half-inch from the top of the page. There are other requirements for APA style headers, which your librarian or the *APA Publication Manual* can help you with. In any case, follow the style set by your instructor or the documentation format you are using.

In most cases, there is no footer in an annotated bibliography. Finally, most instructors want you to include information such as your name, your instructor's name, the course title, and the date at the top of your first page.

3.2.3 Create an Appropriate Title

You will typically not need a title page for your annotated bibliography unless your instructor specifically requests one. You will, however, need a title. The title should be centered at the top of the page and should include "Annotated Bibliography" in it. We suggest the title should also contain your topic as a subtitle. Here is a very simple template:

Annotated Bibliography: My Topic

A variation used in MLA is slightly wordier, but essentially performs the same function of entitling your annotated bibliography:

Annotated List of Works Cited: My Topic

3.2.4 Write the Prefatory Matter

Prefatory matter introduces your research topic and the scope of your research. It should include your proposed thesis statement and purpose.

3.2.5 What Do Annotated Bibliography Entries Look Like?

Each source has its own entry that includes a citation and an annotation. The list will alternate: first a citation of a source, then that source's annotation then the second source, and so on. Add an extra space after each entry and then begin a new citation immediately thereafter.

3.2.6 Length and Word Count

Your annotations should be short, depending on your needs and sources. A typical annotation is 100 words or more. Many instructors recommend that your annotation be between four and six sentences, but an annotation's length will also depend on whether the original source is short or long, and whether you are using the whole source, part of a source, or merely a single fact.

You also need to reword your sources to avoid plagiarism, and this will take more than a thesaurus. Avoiding plagiarism means thinking about what the sources say and composing sentences to tell someone else – *in your own words* – what you find meaningful.

3.2.7 Add the Citations

List sources with all relevant bibliographic information. You can single-space or double-space your entries depending on the format requirements you are following. Your citations must have the **hanging paragraph format** (first line un-indented but all others indented by a half-inch). Line the entries up on the left-hand margin.

Organize your list alphabetically. You should not number the entries unless your instructor specifies otherwise.

At this point, your list of citations will look identical to the way it will look in your final References/Works Cited/Bibliography list at the end of your paper.

3.2.8 Add and Format the Annotations

The margin of the annotation should be indented a half-inch to line up with the indented part of the citation (our preferred method). If your instructor requires, make it flush left.

3.2.9 Check Your Style

The annotated bibliography is semi-formal in style, usually somewhat less formal than the research paper itself. Keep in mind that the annotated bibliography you are writing is for someone else to read. If it is an assignment, that reader is your instructor. Use academic vocabulary. However, it is entirely appropriate to use the first-person "I" in your entries. After all, the entire endeavor is about sources *you* collect, *your* interpretation of those sources, and the way *you* might use them in *your* paper. (See *Chapter 4: Types of Annotations; Chapter 5: Annotating Different Kinds of Sources;* and *Chapter 9: Sample Annotated Bibliographies* for example citations in APA, MLA, and Chicago styles.)

3.3 Guidelines for Writing Your Annotation

3.3.1 Using the Language and Ideas of the Original Text

When you write annotations, you should use your own words to write about the sources. Obviously, the goal for any annotation is to write it as succinctly as possible, such that it will be significantly shorter than the source text. However, in some circumstances, you may want to use an author's exact wording. If you do use an exact **quotation**, copy the quote *exactly* word for word. And, of course, for exact quotations, use quotation marks and follow the guidelines of your style manual for rules about punctuation. In some cases, you may want to **paraphrase** (reword) a passage but not reduce it much in length. Some of the example annotations in this book contain quoted material, and these examples will show you the proper way to document sources if you quote them in an annotation.

3.3.2 To Cite or Not to Cite?

For the most part, you do not need to include in-text citations (or footnotes or numbered notes) in an annotated bibliography. But whenever you include a quote or paraphrase in an annotation, you should indicate a page number. However, *if you want to save time later in your research-writing process*, consider the option of adding an in-text citation to your annotation, which you can later use in your research paper.

3.4 Finished with Your Annotated Bibliography: What Next?

As soon as you have included all your sources, you are done with your annotated bibliography. You probably need to turn it in. But you can re-use it later to work on your paper, so save two copies. Keep one copy of your annotated bibliography itself, and save one copy to cut up later for your research paper (see *Chapter 7: Crunch Time – Annotated Bibliography in Process* for several ways to re-use your annotated bibliography as you write your paper).

3.5 Further Reading

In this chapter, you learned about basic citation and annotation conventions. If you would like to know more, we suggest you look at the following:

Eula, Michael J., and Janet Madden. *Compiling the Annotated Bibliography: A Guide.* Kendall/Hunt Publishing Company, 1995.
Hacker, Diana, and Nancy I. Sommers. *A Pocket Style Manual.* 8th ed., Bedford/ St Martin's, 2018.
Harner, James L. *On Compiling an Annotated Bibliography.* 2nd ed., Modern Language Association of America, 2000.

4
TYPES OF ANNOTATIONS

4.1 Types of Annotations

In working with students on their annotated bibliographies, we have noticed some confusion about how to write a good annotation. As there are many different types of annotations and many kinds of sources, this confusion is understandable. This chapter will guide you through the basics of annotating resources using the five annotation types.

In *Chapter 1: Setting the Stage*, you learned that an annotation is a note about a resource. Annotations are usually written in full sentences and can be very short or very long. The degree of detail you put into your annotation depends on your context and needs.

Here are the five types of annotations:

- Descriptive annotations identify the features and main sections of a source
- Summative annotations recap the main points and arguments of a source
- Evaluative annotations judge the trustworthiness, reliability, and value of a source
- Reflective annotations tell where and how one might use a source in one's work
- Combined annotations use two to four of the annotation types listed above

The sections below explain each of these annotation types in depth.

4.2 Descriptive Annotations

A *descriptive* annotation tells readers about the content and/or composition of a work. It typically lists the basic features of the work, including creators, content, publication format, and other pertinent details. A descriptive annotation should inform your audience about the basic nature of a resource. It can include the following information:

- The work's creators (and facts about said creators)
- Format (e.g., book, artwork, DVD, website, article, etc.)
- Genre (e.g., historical study, literature review, experiment, etc.)
- Nature of material used in the resource (e.g., database, TV ads, clay pottery, etc.)
- Sections, chapters, bibliography, glossary, or other components
- Special features (important tables, figures, diagrams, etc.)
- Primary audience
- Publisher or sponsor
- Length or size
- Anything else important for capturing the nature of the work

As you will see in subsequent sections, all five annotation types need at least a short descriptive sentence (usually mentioning the work's creator and format). This sentence usually appears as the first sentence in any annotation, and it serves to orient your readers.

Think of descriptive annotations as if they were items on a restaurant menu. The menu typically names offerings, lists ingredients, and perhaps specifies how dishes are prepared. Just as a menu names the restaurant offerings, an annotation names the resource by title. Just as a menu categorizes the offerings (e.g., appetizers, entrées, desserts, and drinks), a descriptive annotation identifies the kind of resource being considered. Just as a menu lists ingredients, a descriptive annotation tells what is inside the resource (e.g., sections and illustrations). And just as a menu entry might note how a dish was prepared (e.g., the produce is from local farmers), a descriptive annotation might mention how the resource was created (e.g., it was peer-reviewed).

4.2.1 APA Example of a Descriptive Annotation

Here is a sample descriptive annotation in the American Psychological Association (APA) style for a paper on youth substance abuse:

Justo, L. P., & Calil, H. M. (2016). Relationships between mood disorders and substance abuse during adolescence. In D. D. Micheli, A. L. M. Andrade, E. A. da Silva, M. L. Oliveira, & M. L. O. de Souza Formigoni (Eds.), *Drug abuse in adolescence: Neurobiological, cognitive, and psychological issues* (pp. 173–195). Retrieved from https://is.gd/0bJokH

This book chapter, by Luís Pereira Justo and Helena Maria Calil, is found in the 2016 book *Drug Abuse in Adolescence: Neurobiological, Cognitive, and Psychological Issues*. The chapter is essentially a literature review of the relationships between adolescent mood disorders and substance abuse. The chapter is demarcated by the following sections: "Introduction"; "Mood Disorders"; "Mood Disorders During Adolescence"; "Relationships Between Mood Disorders and Substance Abuse in Adolescents"; and "Conclusion." There are also sub-sections, a reference list, and brief author biographies. Both authors are medical researchers.

4.2.2 MLA Example of a Descriptive Annotation

Here is a descriptive annotation in the Modern Language Association (MLA) style for a paper on The Globe theatre:

Leggatt, Alexander. "Playhouses, Stages and Performances." *Jacobean Public Theatre*, Routledge, 2005, pp. 9–25.

Alexander Leggatt's chapter is found in his 2005 book *Jacobean Public Theatre*. His chapter reviews the history of prominent Jacobean era (1567–1625) playhouses (and associated acting companies) in London. There are eight headings subdividing the chapter: "The Older Playhouses"; "The Boar's Head"; "The Globe"; "The Fortune"; "The Red Bull"; "The Hope"; "Stages"; and "Performances." The chapter also has illustrations and an extensive notes section. The publisher, Routledge, is internationally known and widely regarded as a premier publishing house.

4.2.3 Chicago Example of a Descriptive Annotation

Here is a descriptive annotation in the Chicago style for a paper on the Roman Games:

Potter, David. "Part 4: Roman Games." In *The Victor's Crown: A History of Ancient Sport from Homer to Byzantium*, 163–222. New York, NY: Oxford University Press, 2012.

This book section, entitled *Roman Games*, appears in David Potter's 2012 book *The Victor's Crown: A History of Ancient Sport from Homer to Byzantium*. Potter is a professor of Greek and Roman history. The section contains five chapters: "Greece Meets Rome," wherein the influence of Greece on the Roman games is discussed; "Kings and Games," wherein the influence of high-ranking Roman officials on the Games is discussed; "Rome and Italy," wherein the influence of Italy on the Games is discussed; "Actors and Gladiators," wherein the actors and gladiators are discussed; and "Caesar, Antony, Augustus and the Games," wherein the influence of political figures on the Games is discussed. Potter includes select illustrations, photographs, and extensive notes throughout.

4.2.4 Writing Tips for Descriptive Annotations

Here are a few pointers to make your work easier (see Figure 4.1).

Start with the Author, Title, and Type of Resource

You can usually write one sentence that mentions the author, title, and type of resource. If you can shorten the title, that is recommended.

Look for Key Elements

In descriptive annotations, you want to ensure that you examine all the key elements of the work, and then mention those that seem important. Detail is your friend! Pick apart the resource to find its elements. *Does it have section headings, charts, a table of contents, footnotes, and so on?* Pay attention to the end of the resource. *Is there a bibliography, glossary, index, or appendix?* Each element can help you understand the nature of your resource and, therefore, is an element to consider including in your descriptive annotation. Not all these elements will be important to you, but it is better to err on the side of completeness when first examining the resource, and then to be choosy about what you include in your final descriptive annotation.

Consider Other Factors

While efficiency is good, do not ignore things your instructor would consider important. Maybe you will find something helpful about your source, such as

---

CHECKLIST: Things to Consider for a Descriptive Annotation

☐ Who are the authors or creators?
  ☐ What are their credentials? *Hint: Check for an author biographical statement near the beginning or end of the resource.*
☐ What is the publication format of the work (book, article, website, etc.)?
  ☐ Is it a popular, scholarly, commercial, professional, or governmental resource?
  ☐ Is it peer-reviewed? *Hint: Check the library or the sponsoring organization's website to see if it is peer-reviewed.*
☐ What is the genre of the resource (e.g. historical narrative, sculpture, etc.)?
☐ When was the resource created?
☐ What type of material is used in the resource (including artistic materials)?
☐ What are the main components of the resource?
  ☐ For books, what are the chapters?
  ☐ For articles, what are the section headings?
  ☐ For websites, what are the sub-pages?
  ☐ Does it have a bibliography?
  ☐ Does it have a glossary, table of contents, index, or appendix, etc.?
  ☐ For works of art, what type of material is used to make the art?
☐ Are there special features, such as tables, figures, charts, images, etc.?
☐ Who is the primary audience of the work?
☐ Who published the work? *Hint: Is it a governmental resource, an individual, a professional organization, etc.?*
☐ What is the length or size of the work?
☐ What are any other important factors?

FIGURE 4.1 Descriptive Annotation Checklist.

whether the work reports on a set of 18th-century diaries or draws on statistics from a governmental database. Even the resource's context may be important. For example, if you are describing a book, identify whatever is special about it, such as whether the work is translated or revised from an original. This information will come in handy later if you write an evaluative annotation (which is explained later in this chapter).

Consider Your Own Research Context

When you describe a resource, keep in mind your research context. For example, if your instructor has taken great pains to explain the differences between popular and scholarly sources, it would be a good idea to categorize your source as either popular or scholarly. Depending on your purpose, your familiarity with the topic, and even your instructor's guidelines, you should exclude all but the most critical elements in your description.

Be Concise

You should be concise. Choose the descriptive details that are most important. For example, if you are writing annotations about two articles from the same peer-reviewed journal, you can describe the journal as peer-reviewed for the first annotation, but you do not need to repeat that information in the second annotation.

Work Efficiently

You may be able to write a good descriptive annotation before even reading the resource if you can identify the main parts and satisfy yourself that the source is relevant. Being efficient is important when beginning your research: why waste too much time on a resource if you think you will find other, better sources later? Even if you are not going to fully read the resource until later, you should still describe it adequately.

4.3 Summative Annotations

A summative annotation (sometimes referred to as a "summary annotation") condenses the key points and arguments of a work in your own words. It typically requires an opening sentence describing the work's format and creator, followed by sentences that recap the purpose, theme/thesis, and main points of the work. You may write additional sentences to further explain important supporting points. While it is unusual to include direct quotations in a summative annotation, such inclusion may be warranted when there are important or aptly worded quotations (see *Chapter 3: The Format and Look of the Annotated Bibliography* for guidance on when to quote). Remember, while a *descriptive* annotation lists a work's contents, a *summative* annotation unpacks the content.

Think back to our analogy of the descriptive annotation as being like a restaurant menu, with each menu item specifying the name of the dish and its key ingredients. Similarly, a summative annotation is like a social media post that tells your friends about your dining experience: where you went, what you ate, how you liked the restaurant vibe, and so on. In both cases – the summative annotation and the social media post – the focus is on the highlights of your experience.

4.3.1 APA Example of a Summative Annotation

Here is a summative annotation in the APA style for a paper on youth substance abuse (using the same source we used in the descriptive annotation):

Justo, L. P., & Calil, H. M. (2016). Relationships between mood disorders and substance abuse during adolescence. In D. D. Micheli, A. L. M. Andrade, E. A. da Silva, M. L. Oliveira, & M. L. O. de Souza Formigoni (Eds.), *Drug abuse in adolescence: Neurobiological, cognitive, and psychological issues* (pp. 173–195). Retrieved from https://is.gd/0bJokH

This book chapter, by Justo and Calil, reviews the relationships between adolescent mood disorders and substance abuse. The chapter does not present original research, but rather is an extended literature review. The authors initially discuss the prevalence, (co) morbidities, impacts, and treatment options for adolescents with various mood disorders. They define most of these terms (too long to include here, but they appear on pp. 174–177). Following that, the authors expose a pattern of comorbidity between mood disorders and substance abuse in adults. However, the authors cannot conclude that an equivalent relationship exists with youth/adolescent populations. The authors finally note there is an insufficient literature base addressing research on, or treatment options for, adolescents with mood disorders and substance dependencies.

4.3.2 MLA Example of a Summative Annotation

And here is a summative annotation in the MLA style for a paper on The Globe theatre (using the same source we used in the descriptive annotation):

Leggatt, Alexander. "Playhouses, Stages and Performances." *Jacobean Public Theatre*, Routledge, 2005, pp. 9–25.

Alexander Leggatt's book chapter discusses the prominent playhouses constructed in Jacobean London (1567–1625). In the chapter, Leggatt contends that the playhouses themselves – their location, size, amenities, and so on – were important in getting Londoners out to see a play. In fact, Leggatt argues that the playhouses were more important than the plays, playwrights, or acting companies in drawing audiences. Leggatt provides details about particular theatres and suggests that even the top playhouses of the day had markedly different stage, seating, and design philosophies. These variations allowed for theatres to specialize in different types of productions (clown shows, jigs, dramas, battle scenes, etc.).

4.3.3 Chicago Example of a Summative Annotation

And finally, here is a summative annotation in the Chicago style for a paper on the Roman Games (using the same source we used in the descriptive annotation):

Potter, David. "Part 4: Roman Games." In *The Victor's Crown: A History of Ancient Sport from Homer to Byzantium*, 163–222. New York, NY: Oxford University Press, 2012.

This book section, entitled *Roman Games*, is found in David Potter's book *The Victor's Crown: A History of Ancient Sport from Homer to Byzantium*. The section includes five chapters in which Potter discusses the Roman Games, circa 300 BC-100 AD. Potter touches on activities performed in the Games, including boxing, wrestling, chariot racing, and gladiatorial combat. He also discusses some of the athletes in the Games, including members of the ruling class. In this section, Potter is particularly interested in unpacking the symbolic and political value of the Games, arguing that rulers used the Games to advance regime goals and their own political ends. Finally, he traces the influence of neighboring states, particularly Greece and Italy, on the Games.

4.3.4 Writing Tips for Summative Annotations

Consider What to Include

Writing a summative annotation requires you to identify and reword a work's thesis, purpose, and main points. Finding what is central to the work depends on the type of work it is. For example, if the resource is a factual text written for informative purposes, select the most important points, group similar points in clusters, and then appropriately reword the original work. If your source is argumentative or persuasive, trace the logic to find the author's main claim, main supporting points, main objections raised, and rebuttal to these objections.

Look for useful points such as definitions of key terms for your paper. Avoid quoting long passages in your annotation. Finally, if you catch yourself writing something like, "this work is about …," you are most likely describing the source, not summarizing what the author says.

Consider What to Omit

Summarizing requires you to omit parts of the original work. Sometimes, in fact, you will be interested in only a single point/idea from the work. In this case, focus on your point of interest and briefly describe the remainder of the resource. If the work makes an argument, however, include the author's main claim. If you are uninterested in large portions of a source, you might say something like, "other points raised in this source are not relevant to my work." If you are unsure about how much detail to include in your summary, you can always talk to your instructor.

Consider Your Own Research Context

When you summarize a resource, keep in mind your research context (and your instructor's guidelines). Decide what to include after the main point and purpose of the work. You may or may not need to summarize all the background material, examples, illustrations, or counterarguments the author raises. For example, in summarizing a scientific paper, you would probably mention the method used, but you would summarize that method more fully only if you thought you might use that same method in your work.

Consider Other Factors

Sometimes several resources say much the same thing with only minor differences. If you have already summarized one source but want to use a second source that adds only a little, try to be more efficient in the second summative annotation by emphasizing only new information.

Be Concise

Whatever else is true of summative annotations, they are summaries, and as such they should be as concise as possible. Since you are using your own words, you can condense the work as you see fit. We all know how wordy and technical academic writing can be, so your summary may end up more readable than the original! Using your own words is key. However, if you see a quotation that is particularly apt, go ahead and include it in your summative annotation.

Work Efficiently

For a good summative annotation, you need to consider your source thoroughly to understand it. You can sometimes use a work's organizational structure to help you focus on its main points. For example, scholarly articles first introduce the basic context of an issue and state the author's purpose and thesis; second, they offer a review of prior research (called a literature review, which is a summary of research on a topic); and third, they make an argument of some sort. As another example, scientific reports follow a fixed structure that allows you to zero in on a problem, research question, hypothesis, methods, analysis, findings, and conclusion.

CHECKLIST: Things to Consider for a Summative Annotation

☐ What is the work's subject?
☐ What is the work's purpose – to argue/evaluate, explain/inform, or entertain?
☐ If the resource is written to respond to a problem, what is it?
☐ What is the main thesis or argument?
   ☐ For non-fiction books, what is the main point?
   ☐ For scientific studies, what is the problem, research question, hypothesis, methods, analysis, findings, and conclusion?
   ☐ For arguments, what are the major claims, objections, and rebuttals?
   ☐ For explanatory or informative resources, what is explained?
☐ For fiction:
   ☐ What is the setting and theme?
   ☐ Who are the main characters?
   ☐ What are the main events in the plot?
   ☐ What are important symbols (if any)?
   ☐ What is the climax?
☐ For other creative works, what are the main components (e.g. the main symbols in a poem or a painting)?
☐ Are there any useful facts, definitions, or quotations (and did you remember to cite the page numbers for quotations)?
☐ What can you omit?

FIGURE 4.2 Summative Annotation Checklist.

Avoid Plagiarism

Some students mistakenly think they can cut and paste abstracts from their sources into their summative annotations. Don't do it! That would be stealing, and you would get in trouble. In fact, this would be **plagiarism**, which is the use of someone's work, words, or ideas without acknowledging that person as the source (Figure 4.2).

4.4 Evaluative Annotations

As with other annotation types, the *evaluative* annotation should begin with a very brief description of the work. The purpose of an evaluative annotation, however, is to critique a work. This critique can take many forms, but may include judgments about how convincing the work/research is; the factuality or comprehensiveness of the work; the currency of the work (if in fact currency is important); value of the work to the community; and the credibility of the creator or publisher/sponsor. An evaluative annotation is not necessarily meant to find fault with a work (though it can). It can express praise for, appreciation of, or indifference to the work.

With respect to our restaurant analogy, the evaluative annotation is like talking with your friends after a meal. You might mention the quality of the food, the value of the meal, the restaurant's atmosphere, or even the humorous typos on the menu. In short, each person offers up their judgment about the culinary experience. Likewise, the evaluative annotation is your chance to judge the quality of a resource. In writing an evaluative annotation, you can praise or condemn a work's factuality, currency, readability, artfulness, or importance to the community or profession. Writing an evaluative annotation is also your chance to judge the quality of an author's creativity or thinking, the author's credibility, and the reputation of the publication.

4.4.1 APA Example of an Evaluative Annotation

Here is a sample evaluative annotation in the APA style for a paper on youth substance abuse (using the same source we used in previous annotations):

Justo, L. P., & Calil, H. M. (2016). Relationships between mood disorders and substance abuse during adolescence. In D. D. Micheli, A. L. M. Andrade, E. A. da Silva, M. L. Oliveira, & M. L. O. de Souza Formigoni (Eds.), *Drug abuse in adolescence: Neurobiological, cognitive, and psychological issues* (pp. 173–195). Retrieved from https://is.gd/0bJokH

This book chapter, by Justo and Calil, examines the relationship(s) between adolescent mood disorders and substance abuse. The chapter does not present original research, but rather is a literature review. The chapter is initially helpful in that it gives succinct, clinically informed definitions of adolescence, mood disorders, and substance abuse (pp. 174–177). It then reviews relationships and comorbidities between mood disorders and substance abuse in adult and adolescent populations.

Unfortunately, as the authors point out, the number of studies examining mood disorders and substance abuse in young/adolescent populations is limited as of 2016. If one is willing to accept the authors' contention that adults and adolescents share the commonalities they discuss, this chapter provides several insights regarding the prevalence, impact, and treatment options for adolescents suffering from a combination of mood disorders and substance abuse.

4.4.2 MLA Example of an Evaluative Annotation

And here is an evaluative annotation in the MLA style for a paper on The Globe theatre (using the same source we used in previous annotations):

Leggatt, Alexander. "Playhouses, Stages and Performances." *Jacobean Public Theatre*, Routledge, 2005, pp. 9–25.

This book chapter, by Alexander Leggatt, describes the major playhouses of Jacobean London (1527–1625) and the context in which they operated. Providing succinct, detailed portraits of the major playhouses of the day – The Globe, The Fortune, The Red Bull, and others – Leggatt describes a playgoing experience wherein patrons valued the theatre as much as the plays being performed. Leggatt's evidence for this claim is not wholly convincing, and I believe he undersells the importance of the plays, playwrights, and acting companies in motivating patrons to attend a play. He nonetheless makes a compelling case that Jacobean theatres evolved unique specialties, and that these specialties reflected their size, location, design philosophies, and the expectations of playgoers.

4.4.3 Chicago Example of an Evaluative Annotation

And finally, here is an evaluative annotation in the Chicago style for a paper on the Roman Games (using the same source we used in previous annotations):

Potter, David. "Part 4: Roman Games." In *The Victor's Crown: A History of Ancient Sport from Homer to Byzantium*, 163–222. New York, NY: Oxford University Press, 2012.

This book section, entitled *Roman Games*, is found in David Potter's book *The Victor's Crown: A History of Ancient Sport from Homer to Byzantium*. The section includes five chapters discussing aspects of the Roman Games, circa 300 BCE–100 AD. Taken as a whole, the chapters provide a reasonable overview of the activities, athletes, venues, and spectators. However, Potter is most interested in the symbolic and political value of the Games. Potter argues that the Games provided a unique venue for Roman dignitaries to flaunt their wealth, bolster their popular support, and heighten their reputations. Ultimately, these displays of political dominance over their rivals boosted their standing in high society. The evidence for these claims is extensive and persuasive, and by discussing the political context of the Games, Potter provides a unique lens of analysis.

4.4.4 Writing Tips for Evaluative Annotations

Judge the Value of the Work

In evaluative annotations, your goal is to assess a work's value. Evaluating a work involves four steps. First, judge each component piece of the work on its own merit. Second, judge how well the pieces fit together. Third, evaluate it in light of whatever else you know about the topic. Fourth, note the credibility of the author, publisher, contributors, and so on.

Consider Your Own Research Context

More than anything else, evaluate the work considering your own knowledge and purpose. Does the work make sense given what you know from your experience? Does the work make sense compared to other works you have already evaluated? To write a good evaluative annotation, you need to be watchful and critical of anything in or about the resource that can impact the quality of your own work. After all, if you use a flawed source but never point out its faults, your own work in turn becomes faulty and you risk alienating your audience.

Consider Other Factors

Judge the credibility of the author, other contributors, and possibly the publication itself. Ask, for example, *Is the creator a renowned artist or a tired hack? Does the work appear in an acclaimed journal or a disreputable newspaper known for hyperbole?* Also, think beyond the resource itself. Assess the value of the content in terms of its importance. Ask, *Is this a highly reputable publisher/journal?* and so on.

Work Efficiently But Be Creative

This is your opportunity to praise or even condemn a source. If you find a source with logical flaws, explain the problems. Read between the lines. For example, ascertain whether a writer of an informative or argumentative work has made good or faulty assumptions. When evaluating creative work, use your own aesthetic judgment or a set of relevant disciplinary principles. For example, imagine you have written the description, "This article is from a peer-reviewed journal ..."; now you might add, "so it is from a reputable source" (Figure 4.3).

CHECKLIST: Things to Consider for an Evaluative Annotation

☐ Consider the content of the resource in terms of its value:
  ☐ For argumentative works, how logical is the argument?
  ☐ How factual is the resource (if applicable)? Is it up to date?
  ☐ How comprehensive is the resource?
  ☐ How valid and reliable are the research findings?
  ☐ How important are the conclusions to the discipline or to other relevant communities?
  ☐ For creative works, how well does the work stand up to your aesthetic judgment or disciplinary principles? How original is it (if originality is important)?
☐ How would you rate the method in the source?
  ☐ To what extent are the methods appropriate to the subject?
  ☐ Are the methods carried out well?
☐ How trustworthy is the author or publisher? Is the author or publisher known for expertise or otherwise in a position to be trustworthy?

FIGURE 4.3 Evaluative Annotation Checklist.

4.5 Reflective Annotations

A *reflective* annotation says how, and in what context, one might use a source. You should use a reflective annotation to plan your research. The reflective annotation draws upon all the researcher may have written in other annotations – descriptive, summative, and evaluative – as well as your writing plans. A useful annotation recognizes that "good," "bad," or "mediocre" sources may all be useful for someone's purposes. A source's value is contextual, and its ultimate worth is driven by one's needs (and not simply by the quality of the source).

Returning to our restaurant metaphor, the reflective annotation is like a chat with your friends about where to eat. *What kind of food do we want? What restaurants could we go to? How far are we willing to go?* Similarly, the reflective annotation is your opportunity to plan how and where to use a resource. How much, if any, of the resource's content do you plan to use? How does this resource compare with other resources you have found? If you decide to use this resource, where in the paper would the information fit? Writing this type of annotation is key if you want the annotated bibliography to facilitate your research and not just be a tedious assignment.

4.5.1 APA Example of a Reflective Annotation

Here is a reflective annotation in the APA style for a paper on youth substance abuse (using the same source we used in previous annotations):

Justo, L. P., & Calil, H. M. (2016). Relationships between mood disorders and substance abuse during adolescence. In D. D. Micheli, A. L. M. Andrade, E. A. da Silva, M. L. Oliveira, & M. L. O. de Souza Formigoni (Eds.), *Drug abuse in adolescence: Neurobiological, cognitive, and psychological issues* (pp. 173–195). Retrieved from https://is.gd/0bJokH

> This book chapter, by Justo and Calil, examines the relationships between adolescent mood disorders and substance abuse. Given that I am investigating the effects of opioid use on adolescent depression, this article is quite relevant to my research. Though the article is quite technical, it discusses many types of mood disorders, and the authors pay attention to bipolar disorder (which is a research interest of mine). A particularly helpful section explains that someone who suffers simultaneously from substance abuse and a mood disorder increases the morbidities of both and complicates treatment options for both conditions.
>
> This article also helps clarify my research plans by noting that few scientific studies have examined the relationships between substance abuse and mood disorders in adolescent populations. This means my research could be limited, and I might have to expand my research parameters to include adults.

4.5.2 MLA Example of a Reflective Annotation

And here is a reflective annotation in the MLA style for a paper on The Globe theatre (using the same source we used in previous annotations):

Leggatt, Alexander. "Playhouses, Stages and Performances." *Jacobean Public Theatre*, Routledge, 2005, pp. 9–25.

> Alexander Leggatt's book chapter describes the major playhouses of Jacobean London (1527–1625) and the context in which they operated. As Leggatt notes, very little documentary evidence exists about the playhouses, but he uses the available evidence to good effect. Though my interest is in who attended The Globe and why, I also intend to use information about The Fortune, The Globe's chief competitor. Additionally, I found this chapter's brevity welcome, and the chapter helped me focus on the most essential aspects of the playgoing experience in The Globe. Furthermore, Leggatt claims that patrons valued the playhouse as much as (or more than) the plays being performed, but I think his evidence is unconvincing. I will argue in my paper that Leggatt undersells the importance of any given play, playwright, or actors in attracting patrons.

4.5.3 Chicago Example of a Reflective Annotation

And finally, here is a reflective annotation in the Chicago style for a paper on the Roman Games (using the same source we used in previous annotations):

Potter, David. "Part 4: Roman Games." In *The Victor's Crown: A History of Ancient Sport from Homer to Byzantium*, 163–222. New York, NY: Oxford University Press, 2012.

This book section, entitled *Roman Games*, is found in David Potter's 2012 book. The section includes five chapters discussing aspects of the Roman Games, circa 300 BCE–100 AD. Potter addresses many aspects of the Games that will help me, especially his descriptions of their venues. He also stresses the political and symbolic value of the Games, and because most of my research delves into the nuts and bolts of particular sports (rules, equipment, venues, etc.), Potter's section will provide me excellent contextual material to support my argument.

4.5.4 Writing Tips for Reflective Annotations

Look for Ways to Use the Resource

As you can see in the explanations of the other annotation types, it pays to keep your research plans in mind as you describe, summarize, and evaluate sources. In the reflective annotation, you simply make your plans known to your reader. As a writer, ask yourself first and foremost, *What can I use from this source?* And then, *How and where can I use this in my own work?*

Consider Your Own Research Context

The reflective annotation is about your own research needs. Consider your task, specific instructions from your professor, and anything you have already read or written on the topic. Think about how the potential source relates to your other research. Ask, *Does this resource help me fill a gap in my research? Does it repeat or even bolster ideas brought up in other sources? Does it counter any of the claims made in other sources?* As you reflect upon a particularly useful source, you might consider whether other works by the same creator would be useful to you.

As a final step in your reflection, scan the resource's bibliography (if there is one), and if you see a citation that looks interesting, note it in your reflective annotation. This will remind you of the resource so that you can look it up later.

CHECKLIST: Things to Consider for a Reflective Annotation

☐ What is the work worth in terms of your paper and research needs?
    ☐ For argumentative works, how and where would you use the major claims, evidence, or counterclaims in your paper?
    ☐ For informative works, how and where would the examples, explanations, facts, or definitions fit in your paper?
    ☐ For creative works, how and where might you use its important concepts, including a description of the work itself?
☐ Is the method used in the work one that you might replicate, explain, or criticize in your paper?
☐ If you think a resource is "bad," why and how might you consider using it anyway (e.g., as a counterexample)?
☐ Does this work fit in with your other research?
    ☐ Does this resource fill a gap? If so, how?
    ☐ Does this resource agree or disagree with other resources? If so, how?
    ☐ Is this work irrelevant to your research?
☐ Are other works written by the author or listed in its bibliography potentially useful to you?

FIGURE 4.4 Reflective Annotation Checklist.

Work Efficiently

You do *not* need to repeat what you have said in other annotations; just add to them. In order to do this work efficiently, simply sketch out how and where to use a source. Avoid getting bogged down with the finer details of writing the research paper itself. Keep your reflective annotation concise and ensure you write enough so you understand later what you meant (Figure 4.4).

4.6 Combined Annotations

A *combined* annotation is a mix of the other annotation types. The combined annotation begins with a basic descriptive annotation that, minimally, names the author(s) and the format of the work. It typically includes at least one sentence to summarize the main argument or purpose of a work. After that, a combined annotation goes on to include whatever annotation types you might need. A *combined* annotation is preferable when lengthier analysis is called for.

Going back to our restaurant metaphor, the combined annotation is like a restaurant review. A review names the restaurant and does at least some of the following: it describes the menu; summarizes the dining experience; evaluates the restaurant; and reflectively offers advice to prospective diners. In short, a restaurant review is a critique of the entire restaurant-going experience. In turn, the combined annotation can describe a resource, summarize it, evaluate it, and/or reflect on its potential for use.

The examples below are shorter than typical *combined* annotations might be, but they each describe, summarize, evaluate, and reflect on a resource.

4.6.1 APA Example of a Combined Annotation

Here is a sample combined annotation in the APA style for a paper on youth substance abuse (using the same source we used in the descriptive annotation):

Justo, L. P., & Calil, H. M. (2016). Relationships between mood disorders and substance abuse during adolescence. In D. D. Micheli, A. L. M. Andrade, E. A. da Silva, M. L. Oliveira, & M. L. O. de Souza Formigoni (Eds.), *Drug abuse in adolescence: Neurobiological, cognitive, and psychological issues* (pp. 173–195). Retrieved from https://is.gd/0bJokH

This book chapter, entitled "Relationships Between Mood Disorders and Substance Abuse During Adolescence," by Justo and Calil, is in the 2016 book *Drug Abuse in Adolescence: Neurobiological, Cognitive, and Psychological Issues*. The chapter is a literature review of the relationships between adolescent mood disorders and substance abuse. The authors initially discuss the prevalence, (co)morbidities, impacts, and treatment options for adolescents with various mood disorders. They define most of these terms (too long to include here, but they appear on pp. 174–177). Following that, the authors expose a pattern of significant comorbidity between mood disorders and substance abuse in adults, but they say they cannot conclude the same relationship holds with youth/adolescent populations.

Unfortunately, as the authors point out, the number of studies examining mood disorders and substance abuse in young/adolescent populations is limited as of 2016. If one is willing to accept the authors' contention that adults and adolescents share the commonalities they discuss, this chapter provides a number of insights regarding the prevalence, impact, and treatment options for adolescents suffering from a combination of mood disorders and substance abuse. This article helps clarify my research plans by noting the lack of scientific studies examining the relationships between substance abuse and mood disorders in adolescent populations. I might expand my research parameters to include adult populations.

4.6.2 MLA Example of a Combined Annotation

And here is a combined annotation in the MLA style for a paper on The Globe theatre (using the same source we used in previous annotations):

Leggatt, Alexander. "Playhouses, Stages and Performances." *Jacobean Public Theatre*, Routledge, 2005, pp. 9–25.

This book chapter, entitled *Playhouses, Stages and Performances*, is found in Alexander Leggatt's 2005 book *Jacobean Public Theatre*. The chapter lays out a select history of the most prominent London playhouses and associated acting companies during the Jacobean era (1567–1625). I found this chapter's brevity welcome, and it helped me focus on the most essential aspects of the playgoing experience in The Globe. Providing succinct portraits of the major playhouses of the day – The Globe, The Fortune, The Red Bull, etc. – Leggatt suggests that the top playhouses had markedly different stage, seating, and design philosophies. These variations allowed for theatres to specialize in different types of productions (clown shows, jigs, dramas, battle scenes, etc.). Leggatt also describes a playgoing experience in which the playhouses themselves were as important as the plays, playwrights, and acting companies.

Leggatt's evidence is not wholly convincing, and I also believe he undersells the importance of any given play, playwright, actor, or acting company in attracting an audience. He nonetheless makes a compelling case that Jacobean theatres evolved unique specialties, and that these specialties reflected their size, location, design philosophies, and the expectations of playgoers. Though my research interest is in who attended The Globe and why – which this chapter covers – I also intend to use information Leggatt includes about The Fortune, The Globe's chief competitor.

4.6.3 Chicago Example of a Combined Annotation

And finally, here is a combined annotation in the Chicago style for a paper on the Roman Games (using the same source we used in previous annotations):

Potter, David. "Part 4: Roman Games." In *The Victor's Crown: A History of Ancient Sport from Homer to Byzantium*, 163–222. New York, NY: Oxford University Press, 2012.

This book section, entitled *Roman Games*, is found in David Potter's 2012 book *The Victor's Crown: A History of Ancient Sport from Homer to Byzantium*. The section includes five chapters discussing aspects of the Roman Games, circa 300 BCE–100 AD. Potter touches on activities performed in the Games, including boxing, wrestling, chariot racing, and gladiatorial combat. He also discusses some of the athletes, including members of the ruling class. Potter is particularly interested, however, in unpacking the symbolic and political value of the Games, arguing that rulers used the Games to advance regime goals and their own political ends.

The chapters provide a reasonable overview of the activities, athletes, venues, and spectators who frequented the Games. However, Potter's interest in the symbolic and political value of the Games is interesting. I am especially taken with Potter's argument that the Games provided a unique venue for Roman dignitaries to flaunt their wealth, bolster their popular support, and heighten their reputation. Potter's emphasis on the political dimensions of the Games will provide me with excellent contextual material to support my research. I will not use many of Leggatt's other details, however.

4.6.4 Writing Tips for the Combined Annotation

What to Look For

To know what to write, consult the checklists for descriptive, summative, evaluative, and reflective annotation types.

Work Efficiently

It can be expedient to write your combined annotations in a way that reduces wordiness and redundancy. For example, one sentence might offer both a basic description as well as an evaluation: "This peer-reviewed article reports on a well-conducted survey of 1420 randomly selected parents on their use of punishments and rewards." With that said, think about your needs and decide whether you need to write a few sentences on each annotation type.

CHECKLIST: Things to Consider for a Combined Annotation

- ☐ How detailed does your description need to be?
  - ☐ Have you identified the author and resource format?
  - ☐ Do you need to further describe the resource?
- ☐ To what degree do you need to summarize the resource?
  - ☐ Besides the main thesis and purpose (which you should include no matter what), what supporting details do you need to include?
  - ☐ Are there any details, facts, definitions, or quotes you want to include?
- ☐ To what extent do you need to evaluate the resource?
  - ☐ Is there something important about the author or publisher that affects the work's credibility?
  - ☐ Is there anything about the content you would like to praise or condemn?
- ☐ What can you say as you reflect upon the utility of the resource?
  - ☐ How and/or where might you use it as a source in your work?
  - ☐ If it is a "bad" source, is there a good way to use it?
- ☐ Can you write annotations of each type in only a sentence or two, or do you need to go into more depth?
- ☐ Have you used the other four annotation type checklists to guide you?

FIGURE 4.5 Combined Annotation Checklist.

Consider Your Own Research Context

When writing a combined annotation, keep in mind your research purposes and your other sources. But there is no hard-and-fast rule! Write as much or as little as you need (Figure 4.5).

4.7 Final Advice

In this chapter, you have learned how to write five annotation types: descriptive, summative, evaluative, reflective, and combined. We have explained their key features and objectives, and we have given you tips on how to create them. Along the way, we mentioned some key points:

- Keep your purpose and task in mind
- Consider your instructor's directions and your professional or academic context
- Remember to write annotations whose length depends on the nature of the resource and your needs

- Use the five annotation types flexibly, selecting a combination of the first four types appropriately
- Use the checklists in this chapter

The foremost thing to remember when working on an annotated bibliography is that you should pay close attention to your context and purpose. The more you consider how you will use the works as sources in your paper, the more clear-headed you will be about what to include in your annotations. That will make you more efficient, and your annotated bibliography will be more useful later.

As you continue to work, use the annotated bibliography as a way of keeping track of your research, especially regarding who says what, what points are repeated across sources, who disagrees with whom, and what subtopics you still need to research.

Pay attention to your instructor's guidelines. Your instructor may or may not give you specific guidelines on the type of annotations to write, the length of annotations expected, or the content to include in your annotations. Your instructor may even use slightly different vocabulary from ours. For example, some instructors will tell you to "write a critical annotation," which, in our experience, can mean any combination of descriptive, summative, evaluative, and/or reflective annotations. If you are unsure of what to write, ask!

If, on the other hand, you are given the freedom to write your annotated bibliography as you wish, you can concentrate on annotating in the way you deem most useful. In this scenario, it is up to you to determine which annotation types are the ones to write. Usually, however, you should include a few sentences to describe and summarize the resource. Adding your evaluation of the work and your reflection on its utility will help you in later stages.

While it is important to understand *how* to write an annotation, it is also important to understand *when* to write it.

At the very beginning of your research process, stick to writing descriptive and evaluative annotations to get a sense of direction for your paper. Then, as you begin to get a clearer idea of what your paper is going to say, you can be more comprehensive by adding summative annotations. Until you are far enough in your research, however, you may not know enough to write a reflective annotation because you do not yet have a clear plan for your paper. Once you envision your paper taking shape and you think of a way to use a source, write a reflective annotation right away.

As you become more of an expert on your topic, you also become more judicious about what to include in your annotations. For example, you might more easily recognize that a given source is better or worse than other sources you have already annotated. If you are annotating a source and conclude you will not use it, write an evaluative annotation and a reflective annotation to explain why. As another example, if a resource repeats what another source says, maybe all you need to do is note that redundancy and emphasize what is unique about this new source.

Especially in more advanced courses, your writing needs to use appropriate disciplinary conventions. For more detail on creating annotations in various professions and academic fields, you will want to have a look at *Chapter 5: Annotating Different Kinds of Sources*, where we detail how to annotate a variety of different resource types (books, articles, websites, videos, etc.) in different disciplines.

4.8 Further Reading

If you would like to read more about annotated bibliographies, consider the following:

Colaianne, Anthony Joseph. "The Aims and Methods of Annotated Bibliography." *Scholarly Publishing*, vol. 11, no. 4, 1980, pp. 321–331.

Eula, Michael J., and Janet Madden. *Compiling the Annotated Bibliography: A Guide.* 2nd ed., Kendall/Hunt Pub. C., 1995.

Harner, James L. *On Compiling an Annotated Bibliography.* 2nd ed., Modern Language Association of America, 2000.

5

ANNOTATING DIFFERENT KINDS OF SOURCES

5.1 Introduction

In this chapter, we will give you some tips on annotating various kinds of sources. We will also provide you with example annotations. The sources we will work with in this chapter are among the most common ones used by students and other researchers:

- Books
- Book chapters/sections
- Journal articles
- Magazine articles
- Newspaper articles
- Encyclopedia articles/entries
- Blogs/podcasts
- Websites/webpages
- Videos/films/TV shows
- Government reports/technical reports
- Images/art/music
- Dissertations

For demonstration purposes, all the example annotations we include in this chapter are accessible to anyone with an Internet connection. However, if you are seeking sources for a research project, you can access much more material through academic or public libraries.

5.2 Books

Below you will find some tips for annotating books as well as sample annotations to guide you.

5.2.1 Book Annotation Tips

- If you plan to use an entire book for your research, you might consider using a *combined* annotation, as the book will typically contain a large amount of information (relative to other types of research sources).
- Sometimes you might be working with an edited book, which means the book has a different set of authors for each chapter and editors for the book. In this case, you might consider annotating just the chapter(s) you plan to use in your research (see the section on annotating book chapters below).
- If you are annotating a fiction book, ensure that your annotation contains a brief precis of the plot, and concentrate the bulk of your effort on evaluative and reflective annotations.

5.2.2 Sample Book Annotations

Here is a sample American Psychological Association (APA) citation and annotation for a paper on international criminal courts.

Fichtelberg, A. (2015). *Hybrid tribunals: A comparative examination.* New York: Springer. Retrieved from https://is.gd/ld1gda

In this book, Fichtelberg discusses the creation and organization of hybrid tribunals. Hybrid tribunals are pseudo-international courts that "represent a unique development in the history of international law ... hybrid courts have sought to integrate foreign laws and personnel [judges] with domestic ones to different degrees and to different extents" (vii). The hybrid tribunals discussed are the Special Court for Sierra Leone (SCSL), the Extraordinary Chambers in the Courts of Cambodia (ECCC), the Serious Crimes Panel, Dili (SCPD), the Bosnia War Crimes Chamber (BWCC), the United Nations Interim Administration Mission in Kosovo (UNMIK) Court, and the Special Tribunal for Lebanon (STL).

Though hybrid tribunals are not fully international courts – they draw some of their laws, judges, and practices from particular countries – they are an important variation of the international court. Fichtelberg's book is clearly written, but it includes more detail and

> specificity than I need for my paper. Aside from the cases he dis-
> cusses, I will also draw good background information from his intro-
> ductory and concluding chapters.

Here is a sample Modern Language Association (MLA) citation and annotation for a paper on ancient Greek theatre.

> Puchner, Walter, and Andrew Walker White. *Greek Theatre between Antiquity and Independence: A History of Reinvention from the 3rd Century BC To 1830*. Cambridge University Press, 2017, https://is.gd/wZtFqq
>
> This book, by Walter Puchner and Andrew Walker White, chronicles the history of Greek theatre from the third century BCE to AD 1830. The authors provide a fulsome and well-referenced account in the book's eight chapters, with each chapter addressing a period of Greek theatre. Instead of arguing that Greek theatre evolved linearly, Puchner and White rather suggest that "[the history of Greek theatre] must be narrated by focusing on discrete, independent times and places, each of which operates along its own unique lines" (p. viii).
>
> Though the prose in this book is a bit heavy, and many of the later chapters are not relevant to my research, the earlier chapters in the book are invaluable for my paper. Though I am still early in my research, I was surprised to learn how profoundly the Orthodox Church impacted Greek theatre after the seventh century, and I will certainly research this phenomenon more.

Here is a sample Chicago citation and annotation for a paper on World War II Allied propaganda.

> Husband, Tony, ed. 2013. *Cartoons of World War II*. London: Arcturus. https://is.gd/SWVlUk
>
> In this book, Tony Husband compiles a series of black and white World War II propaganda cartoons. The book is laid out in a straightforward manner, with a distinct chapter given to each of the war years (1939–1945) and to a pre-war period. The book features both Allied and Axis cartoons, emphasizing cartoons produced in America, Russia, Britain, and Germany. I did not see many cartoons from Italy or Japan.

The cartoons in this book are powerful and affecting, and I will use several them in my paper. But the book is otherwise useless to me because, outside of an introductory chapter, Husband provides very little context or exposition. Though I imagine there is a story/narrative that Husband is trying to develop through these cartoons, it is not immediately clear what that might be.

5.3 Book Chapters/Sections

Below you will find some tips for annotating book chapters as well as sample annotations to guide you.

5.3.1 Book Chapter Annotation Tips

- The book chapter lends itself well to all annotation types. For longer or more important chapters, a combined annotation might be warranted.
- Sometimes you might be working with an edited book. In this case, consider annotating just the chapter(s) you plan to use in your research (see the section on annotating edited books, above). Ensure you correctly cite the authors and titles of your chosen chapter(s).
- If you plan to use only a single chapter from a (non-edited) book, you can annotate that single chapter and note in your annotation that the remainder of the book was irrelevant to your research needs.

5.3.2 Sample Book Chapter Annotations

Here is a sample APA citation and annotation for a paper on the chemistry of coffee.

Satin, M. (2011). The chemistry and health benefits of coffee. In *Coffee talk: The stimulating story of the world's most popular brew* (pp. 65–88). Retrieved from https://is.gd/4omg9w

This book chapter, by Satin, addresses chemical properties of coffee and potential effects of coffee on human health. Satin's writing is direct and jargon-free. Following an introduction about the chemical properties of coffee beans, Satin organizes his chapter into four sections: "How Roasting Changes Coffee's Composition," "Tasting Coffee," "Coffee and Health," and "Benefits of Coffee Consumption." The latter two sections interest me the most, as they summarize decades of research on caffeine and coffee's relationship to health. Because Morton's book is written for a general reader, the chemical discussion is elementary, so I can use some of this information in my paper's background section.

Here is a sample MLA citation and annotation for a paper on authors and copyright issues.

Lavik, Erlend. "Romantic Authorship in Copyright Law and the Uses of Aesthetics." *The Work of Authorship*, edited by Mireille Van Eechoud, Amsterdam University Press, 2015, pp. 45–93, https://is.gd/qlJpJJ

In this densely written book chapter, Erlend Lavik argues that notions of Romantic authorship are deeply ingrained in US and EU copyright law. Lavik contends that Romantic authorship privileges the idea that authors are less the sum of their influences and more the product of their individual genius and inspiration. Thus, Lavik argues, a Romantic notion of authorship is one in which an author can claim sole authorship of a work and thereby profit from that ownership. Prior to the Romantic period, Lavik argues, authors were not as concerned with establishing the originality of their ideas.

I found this chapter quite difficult to read, but ultimately, I found Lavik's linking of Romantic authorship and its effect on copyright law convincing. The second half of this chapter, which I did not read, apparently deals with ways that humanities can inform current copyright debates. It is irrelevant to my research and seemed like a slog, so I moved on.

Here is a sample Chicago citation and annotation for a paper on biblical ethics.

Davies, Eryl W. "The Bible in Ethics." In *The Oxford Handbook of Biblical Studies*, edited by J. W. Rogerson and Judith M. Lieu, 732–753. New York, NY: Oxford University Press, 2006. https://is.gd/C0YD0o

This book chapter, by Eryl Davies, discusses common approaches to and issues of studying biblical ethics. Four sections subdivide this chapter: "Methodological Issues," "The Basis of Old Testament Ethics," "New Testament Ethics," and "Hermeneutical Issues." Davies' writing is accessible given the subject material. A theme that Davies returns to throughout chapter is the sheer *volume* of material in the Old and New Testaments with which scholars must contend; I had not previously considered this issue. This chapter is excellent as both an overview and a substantive source, and it will save me time because I can focus my research on the four trouble spots Davies identifies.

5.4 Journal Articles

Below you will find some tips for annotating journal articles as well as sample annotations to guide you.

5.4.1 Journal Article Annotation Tips

- Along with books, journal articles are the most used sources in academia. Learning how to read an academic article is an important skill for succeeding in your studies. See *Chapter 6: Composing Your Annotations* for tips on summarizing a journal article.
- Journal articles can be annotated using all five of the different annotation types, but we have noticed that professors from science disciplines tend to like their students to do descriptive and summative annotations, while professors in the humanities tend to prioritize evaluative and reflective annotations (preferring the descriptions and summaries to be brief).
- Most students get their journal articles from library databases or *Google Scholar*, which have built-in citation tools. The citations they generate are not always perfect, but they are typically pretty good, so consider grabbing your citation at the source rather than creating it from scratch later. If you cannot find a citation through a database, see *Chapter 7: Crunch Time – Annotated Bibliography in Process* for a list of citation tools.

5.4.2 Sample Journal Article Annotations

Here is a sample APA citation and annotation for a paper on landscaping on college campuses.

Speake, J., Edmondson, S., & Nawaz, H. (2013). Everyday encounters with nature: Students' perceptions and use of university campus green spaces. *Human Geographies – Journal of Studies and Research in Human Geography*, *7*(1), 21–31. Retrieved from https://is.gd/chWnxx

This journal article, by Speake et al., investigates how students use green spaces at Liverpool Hope University. Green spaces are taken to be lawns, sporting fields, and naturalistic areas on campus. The authors used a three-page questionnaire administered to 205 undergraduate and postgraduate students. Approximately half of the respondents indicated that they used the campus green spaces. Socializing and relaxing were the two most cited activities that students engaged in on the green space. The proximity of the green spaces to the students' place of residence was noted to be important in their choice of space.

> In this study, as in my other research, green spaces that were too wild or too manicured were rated less positively than nicely-maintained-but-still-natural-looking green spaces. Though this study is limited to a single environment, I can draw from it to supplement my existing research on higher education landscaping.

Here is a sample MLA citation and annotation for a paper on using digital humanities with classic texts.

Gazzoni, Andrea. "Mapping Dante: A Digital Platform for the Study of Places in the Commedia." *Humanist Studies & the Digital Age*, vol. 5, no. 1, 2017, pp. 83–96, https://is.gd/1B6PLb

This journal article, by Andrea Gazzoni, reports on her project of mapping out all the place-names in Dante's *The Divine Comedy*. Using the *ArcGIS* technology, Gazzoni published an online map (www.mapping dante.com/) which identifies the place-names with a digital pin. The map also features several layers that allow the user to filter the pins by a variety of criteria. Gazzoni notes that arranging a text cartographically allows for new methods of analysis and understanding. As I am interested in how digital humanities can breathe new life into classic works, I found this article to be useful for my research program. I will discuss mapping/GIS technologies in my paper, and this article will feature heavily in my discussion.

Here is a sample Chicago citation and annotation for a paper on American Buddhist practices.

Choe, Jaeyeon, and John McNally. "Buddhism in the United States: An Ethnographic Study." *International Journal of Religious Tourism and Pilgrimage* 1, no. 1 (2013). https://is.gd/DYKzEH

In this journal article, Jaeyeon Choe and John McNally describe an ethnographic study in which they joined an American Buddhist meditation group for four months in 2010. This meditation group had 12 members, but only three of them were practicing Buddhists. The authors aptly describe the practices, rituals, and social dynamics of this group, but they fail to provide a larger ethnography of American Buddhism, as the article title suggests they might.

Regardless, there is a literature review in the article addressing the nature of Buddhist practices and thought in 20th–21st-century America, and this will be quite useful for my paper. In the literature review, the authors contend that the non-religious and therapeutic aspects of Buddhism have been co-opted into America's commercialized self-help and self-healing industries, and I thought this would be an interesting angle for my paper. I might look up some of the authors cited in the literature review.

5.5 Encyclopedia Articles/Entries

Below you will find some tips for annotating encyclopedia articles/entries as well as sample annotations to guide you.

5.5.1 Encyclopedia Articles/Entries Annotation Tips

*   Because many encyclopedia articles contain background or foundational information, they lend themselves well to descriptive and summative annotations.
*   Because the information in a typical encyclopedia article is highly vetted and uncontroversial, an evaluative annotation beyond noting the trustworthiness of an encyclopedia would be unnecessary.
*   If you are working with an article from an edited encyclopedia and the entries have identified authors, ensure you are correctly citing the article's author. Many encyclopedia entries do not name an author, so for these you will cite the article's title in lieu of an author.

5.5.2 Sample Encyclopedia Article/Entry Annotations

Here is a sample APA citation and annotation for a paper on the aviation industry.

Lagasse, P. (2006). Airline industry. In C. R. Geisst (Ed.), *Encyclopedia of American business history* (Vol. 1, pp. 9–12). Retrieved from https://is.gd/DC8Eh8

This encyclopedia entry, by Lagasse, gives a brief history of the American airline industry from the mid-1910s to the post-9/11 period. Aside from assembling a variety of statistics and factoids, Lagasse accounts for how the federal government regulated the industry up through the 1970s and argues that the regulations shaped all facets of air travel. Although this article is a bit dated, I found Lagasse's history

> well written, and I will refer to some of his insights on federal govern-
> ment regulation in my paper. I will not use any of Lagasse's statistics,
> as I can find more updated figures elsewhere.

Here is a sample MLA citation and annotation for a paper on country-western music.

> Cohen, Norm. "The Folk and Popular Roots of Country Music." *The Encyclope-
> dia of Country Music*, edited by Paul Kingsbury et al., 2nd ed.,
> Oxford University Press, 2012, pp. 176–180, https://is.gd/nsOqzL
>
> This encyclopedia article, by Norm Cohen, discusses how folk/hillbilly
> music influenced the development of country music. The article con-
> tains sections on the following types of musical performance: minstrel,
> Tin Pan Alley, ragtime, jazz, and gospel. Following that, the article
> speculates on the influence popular records and sheet-music had on
> country performers. The article lists key performers and songs in each
> musical genre, and I imagine the sections on ragtime and jazz will be
> useful for my paper because I have not encountered much discussion
> of those genres in my research so far.

Here is a sample Chicago citation and annotation for a paper on African creation myths.

> Bankole, Katherine Olukemi. 2009. "Creation." In *Encyclopedia of African Reli-
> gion*, edited by Molefi Kete Asante and Ama Mazama, 184–186.
> Thousand Oaks, Calif: SAGE. https://is.gd/NBAfiQ
>
> This encyclopedia entry, by Bankole, gives an overview of African cre-
> ation narratives, which the author describes as "the origins of the sky,
> man, plants, animals, and the earth" (p. 184). Though readily
> acknowledging that African creation narratives are disparate, the
> author draws together some commonalities from across the African
> diaspora, and argues that *most* African creation myths contain the fol-
> lowing elements: (1) a self-existing God or Gods who create the uni-
> verse; (2) lesser deities who aid the God or Gods; (3) ancestral spirits;
> and (4) elemental/natural spirits.
>
> Bankole asserts that life/death cycles and agricultural yields are par-
> ticularly associated with supernatural action. Bankole also notes that

the effects of colonialism on African creation narratives are still poorly understood. The bulk of my research has thus far focused on sub-Saharan creation myths, so this article will provide a nice, if preliminary, summary of other African creation narratives. I plan to seek out more information on many of Bankole's ideas.

5.6 Magazine Articles

Below you will find some tips for annotating magazine articles as well as sample annotations to guide you.

5.6.1 Magazine Article Annotation Tips

- A magazine article is typically less structured than a journal article, and your annotation can be different when it comes to evaluating the worth or value of the article. Elements such as writing style, ability to maintain interest, aesthetics, and so on might matter to your instructor or audience. Regardless, if you do an evaluative annotation, ensure you judge the substance of the article.
- Magazine articles often eschew sections/subheadings, and if this is the case with your article, you should prioritize summative, evaluative, or reflective annotations because there won't be a lot of "bullet points" to describe anyway.
- Magazine articles can be more openly opinionated/ideological than journal articles. It is worth noting somewhere in your annotation if you think this is the case.

5.6.2 Sample Magazine Article Annotations

Here is a sample APA annotation for a paper on the rhetoric of the Tea Party.

Gupta, A. (October 20, 2010). The Tea Party of no. *The Indypendent, 157,* 8–9, 12. Retrieved from https://is.gd/y4FgLX

In this short magazine article, journalist Gupta argues that the Tea Party movement has gained political capital through its use of populist rhetoric. Gupta notes that the Tea Party has positioned itself as the guardian of a besieged middle class, and he says that in their self-appointed role as defenders of the people, they have made it a point to undermine progressives. Gupta argues that the Tea Party's "no!" ethos (no welfare, no immigrants, no socialism, etc.) undermines progressive causes through appeals to neo-corporate and capitalist values.

Gupta's characterization of the Tea Party is politicized, but his arguments are convincing. I especially appreciate his chilling discussion of how the Tea Party demonizes immigrants, non-whites, and homosexuals. Though the article is brief, it discusses the Tea Party's philosophical forebears (1960s conservatives Barry Goldwater and George Wallace), and I think this history will be useful in discussing the rhetorical precursors to the Tea Party.

Here is a sample MLA annotation for a paper on Japanese science fiction films.

Shoemaker, Greg. "Daiei: A History of the Greater Japan Motion Picture Company." *The Japanese Fantasy Film Journal*, vol. 12, 1979, pp. 10–15, https://is.gd/831XYa

This magazine article, by Greg Shoemaker, chronicles the history of the Daiei Film Company. Incorporated in 1942, the studio rose to prominence following World War II under the guidance of studio president Masaichi Nagata, who prioritized making films for the foreign market. Shoemaker argues that this goal led the studio to be technically innovative with their films, but that it also led them to film unambitious scripts that would profit in foreign markets.

Though this article gives a readable history of the Daiei company, it *barely* touches on the prominent science fiction franchises the studio was known for. As such, I do not imagine I will use a lot from this article in my paper. I will use only the part where Shoemaker discusses how the Daiei company produced juvenile material and science fiction/fantasy in the 1960s to capitalize on market trends. I can tie this in with some broader trends in Japanese film at the time. Though this publication is a journal in name, it is a newsletter in spirit: Shoemaker writes all the articles, and he hardly refers to outside sources.

Here is a Chicago annotation for a paper on the Edsel.

Roberts, Bruce D. 2013. "Ford Fiasco: Tracking the Rise and Fall of the Edsel in American Newspaper Archives." *Readex Report* 8 (3). https://is.gd/yELqpQ

This magazine article, by Bruce D. Roberts, tracks the rise and fall of the Edsel. This article is unique in that it incorporates primary source materials – mostly newspapers – to add color to Roberts' narrative.

Coverage of the Edsel begins in the mid-1950s and concludes in 1960, when production of the Edsel ceased. Though I have other sources chronicling the Edsel's production history, this source stands out by illustrating how newspapers covered the Edsel (not favorably). I found it interesting to see how the media's coverage soured over the years, and I would like to bring that insight into my paper.

5.7 Newspaper Articles

Below you will find some tips for annotating newspaper articles as well as sample annotations to guide you.

5.7.1 Newspaper Article Annotation Tips

- Newspaper articles briefly report or comment on a piece of contemporary news. Summative or reflective annotations are usually your best bet for newspaper articles, but if the reporting seems shaky, check the facts with alternative sources.
- Newspapers can also include investigative reports, journalistic exposés, and longer feature articles; for these, evaluative annotations may be appropriate because these articles can significantly contribute to the conversation on a given issue.
- Chances are you will be reading an online newspaper. If in doubt about how to cite this, ask a librarian, use an online citation generator, or consult your style manual.

5.7.2 Sample Newspaper Article Annotations

Here is a sample APA citation and annotation for a paper on the impact of soda on childhood obesity.

Tanner, L. (May 14, 2019). Philadelphia's soda tax has reduced soft-drink sales, study says, and raised $130M for preschool. *Chicago Tribune*. Retrieved from https://is.gd/WG94WP

This newspaper article from the *Chicago Tribune* reports on Philadelphia's "soda tax," which since 2017 has generated over $130 million in revenue and has resulted in a 38% decline in soda pop sales. In addition to interviewing city officials and local business owners, the author reports on a research study which analyzed the soda tax. The study concludes that, since the advent of the tax, sales volume of soda pop and sugary drinks in Philadelphia has declined by 1.3 billion ounces. The study's authors were unable to conclude that this decline had a tangible health benefit for Philadelphians, though. I plan to use this article to demonstrate that soda taxes can help dramatically reduce soda consumption.

Here is a sample MLA citation and annotation for a paper on modern adaptations of *Beowulf*.

Flood, Alison. "JRR Tolkien Translation of Beowulf to Be Published after 90-Year Wait." *The Guardian*, March 19, 2014. *www.theguardian.com*, https://is.gd/WlzDVv

This newspaper article, published in *The Guardian*, reports on the posthumous 2014 publication of J.R.R. Tolkien's translation of the epic poem *Beowulf*. Much of the article features an interview with Tolkien's son, Christopher, who edited the translation. The remainder of the article discusses the context of Tolkien's translation (he completed it in 1926), the impact that *Beowulf* had on Tolkien's other work (considerable), and the critical reception of Tolkien's translation (mixed-to-negative). I plan to use this article in my paper because of the interview with Christopher Tolkien and the article's discussion of why it took the translation so long to be published.

Here is a sample Chicago citation and annotation for a paper on the history of Internet browsers.

Campbell, W. Joseph. "The Rise and Fall of Netscape." *The Baltimore Sun*, August 8, 2016. https://is.gd/eqKWfx

This newspaper article, published in *The Baltimore Sun*, gives a brief history of the Internet browser *Netscape*. The article touches on four key points in *Netscape*'s history: the browser's origins in 1994; its initial public offering of shares in 1995; its technological innovations in the mid-1990s (JavaScript and Secure Sockets being the biggest); and its eventual loss to Microsoft in the browser wars of the late 1990s. Though *Netscape* is not a focus of my paper – *Firefox* and *Chrome* are the two browsers I will mainly write on – the fact that *Netscape* was a precursor to modern web browsers makes it historically significant. I can use this article to refer to the key points of the browser's history.

5.8 Blogs/Podcasts

Below you will find some tips for annotating blogs/podcasts as well as sample annotations to guide you.

5.8.1 Blog/Podcast Annotation Tips

- Blogs and podcasts are uniquely online formats, but many lack an editor to oversee the quality of their content. At least some of your annotation should be given over to evaluating the worth or value of these sources.
- Owing to the personal and idiosyncratic nature of some blogs/podcasts, they can be excellent anthropological snapshots of a culture or society. Ensure that your descriptive and summative annotations provide your reader enough context to understand the significance of the source.
- With podcasts, you may be able to find a written transcription which can help you with quoting and paraphrasing information from that podcast.

5.8.2 Sample Blog/Podcast Annotations

Here is a sample APA citation and annotation for a paper on Girl Scouts.

Dubner, S. J. (Presenter). (July 17, 2019). What do Nancy Pelosi, Taylor Swift, and Serena Williams have in common? (Ep. 385) [Audio Podcast]. In *Freakonomics*. Retrieved from https://is.gd/Cc88od

This podcast, hosted by Stephen Dubner, features an interview with Sylvia Acevado, who is the CEO of the Girl Scouts. Much of the interview is given over to Acevado's background leading up to her tenure as CEO. About halfway through the podcast's 40-minute runtime, the interview turns to the Girl Scouts, and Acevado addresses several issues facing the Girl Scouts (declining membership, politicization of the troops, the business pressures of selling cookies, etc.). I found the latter half of the interview was relevant to my research, but the first half was a complete write-off. Also, the podcast title could not have been more misleading – not a single mention of Nancy Pelosi, Taylor Swift, or Serena Williams in the entire podcast!

Here is a sample MLA citation and annotation for a paper on Italian literature.

Hainsworth, Peter. "From Dante to Umberto Eco: Why Read Italian Literature?" *OUPblog*, Oxford University Press, June 8, 2012, https://is.gd/PryUgz

> In this blog, Peter Hainsworth argues that Italian literature and poetry are not more widely read owing to three factors: (1) that classical Italian works were often written in literary Tuscan, a language unspoken and unreadable by Italian commoners and foreigners; (2) that literary Tuscan favored a style of "abstraction and generalization" and thus confounded many translators and would-be readers; and (3) that Italians were notoriously slow to adopt the novel as a literary form. Hainsworth, who authored the 2012 book *Italian Literature: A Very Short Introduction*, argues that, while modern Italian literature has found an international audience, that same audience might also find classical Italian works rewarding as well.

Here is a sample Chicago citation and annotation for a paper on binge watching.

Linsenmayer, Mark. July 23, 2019. "Pretty Much Pop #2: Binge Watching." Podcast audio. *The Partially Examined Life: A Philosophy Podcast and Philosophy Blog*. The Partially Examined Life, LLC. Accessed July 29, 2019. https://is.gd/GgYqnx

> This podcast, hosted by Mark Linsenmayer, features an interview about binge watching with actor/musician Erica Spyres and writer/linguist Brian Hirt. The podcast begins with the trio discussing various statistics about television and media consumption, and soon the discussion turns to the practice of binge watching. The trio discuss aspects of the binge-watching experience, but the highlight for me was an extended discussion on how binge watching compares to other forms of passive entertainment (similarly, they argue).
>
> The trio make a fruitful comparison between erstwhile attitudes about novel reading (anti-social, indulgent, solipsistic, etc.) and modern attitudes about binge watching (lazy, obsessive, undisciplined, etc.). I had not considered any of this! I cannot say for sure whether I will use information from this podcast, but at the very least, it has given me the idea to directly compare binge watching with other forms of passive entertainment.

5.9 Websites/Webpages

Below you will find some tips for annotating websites and webpages as well as sample annotations to guide you.

5.9.1 Website/Webpage Annotation Tips

- A **webpage** is a single page/document on the Internet; a **website** is a collection of webpages. If the website were a house, the webpages would be the rooms in the house.
- You will typically want to focus on descriptive or reflective annotations when annotating websites (especially large ones) owing to the sheer volume of their content. Effectively summarizing or evaluating *all* the content on a website can be very difficult.
- As webpages vary, you could theoretically employ any of the five annotation types to annotate your page, though you should always give your readers some context about the larger website.

5.9.2 Sample Website/Webpage Annotations

Here is a sample APA citation and annotation for a paper on Richard Fenyman's influence on physics.

Feynman, R., Leighton, R., & Sands, M. (2013). The Feynman Lectures on Physics. Retrieved July 29, 2019, from https://is.gd/IV8iuh

Richard Fenyman's most prolific work was his compiled lecture series *The Fenyman Lectures on Physics*, published in three volumes from 1961 to 1963. This webpage offers a digital version of those volumes, as well as photos and notes from the lecture series. Each volume – "Volume I: Mainly Mechanics, Radiation, and Heat," "Volume II: Mainly Electromagnetism and Matter," and "Volume III: Quantum Mechanics" – has 20–50 chapters. Because of searchability and the sheer weight of the physical volumes, it is reasonable to assume that many students would choose to read this version of Fenyman's lectures. In my paper, I will comment on the benefits and drawbacks of the digital version of Fenyman's lectures, as compared to the print volumes.

Here is a sample MLA citation and annotation for a paper on Aaron Copland.

Library of Congress. "A Brief Introduction to the Music of Aaron Copland." Library of Congress 2019, https://is.gd/gjljD4

This webpage, created by the Library of Congress, contains seven mini-essays about Aaron Copland's life. Within each essay are numerous links to digital items held in the Library of Congress' *Aaron Copland Collection* (a collection of ~1,000 digital objects pertaining to Copland's life and music). The writing in the mini-essays is concise and to the point, and each of the essays is thematically coherent. As the essays cover the breadth of Copland's life and there are so many linked objects embedded in the essays, I have not yet decided which of these items I will use in my paper.

Here is a sample Chicago citation and annotation for a paper on modern devotional literature.

Harvard Divinity School. "Four Principles: Differentiating Between Devotional Expression and the Study of Religion." Religious Literacy Project, 2019. https://is.gd/Lv0Cl7

This brief essay, by the Harvard Divinity School, outlines four key differences between the *study* of religion and the *devotional expression* of religion. The differences are as follows:

- Religious scholars consider the validity of many religious claims, while devotional practitioners discount the claims of competing religions.
- Religious scholars view religions as "internally diverse," while devotional practitioners tend to conceive of a given religion as uniform.
- Religious scholars acknowledge that religions evolve, while devotional practitioners often express religious belief through unchanging and decontextualized normative rituals.
- Religious scholars contend that religion is inseparable from cultural and political influences, while many devotional practitioners operate in a private context that does not recognize the influence of culture and politics on their faith.

This essay will help me in the background sections of my paper where I will define what "devotional" is (and can be).

5.10 Videos/Films/TV Shows

Below you will find some tips for annotating videos/films/TV shows as well as sample annotations to guide you.

5.10.1 Video/Film/TV Show Annotation Tips

- Outside of documentaries, most videos/films/TV shows are for entertainment, so a summative, evaluative, or reflective annotation can work together to capture the essence of the work and why you might use it.
- Documentaries, however, are essentially essays-put-to-video, and many have a profound impact on the understanding of a topic. Because of this, you should evaluate the work in some manner.
- Producing citations for visual materials is notoriously complex. If you are unsure how to cite these materials, ask a librarian, use an online citation generator, or consult your style manual.

5.10.2 Sample Video/Film/TV Show Annotations

Here is a sample APA citation and annotation for a paper on machine learning.

Arora, S., & Institute for Advanced Study. (2019). *Brief introduction to deep learning and the "Alchemy" controversy* [Online video]. Retrieved from https://is.gd/yajq2t

In this lecture, Sanjeev Arora (a computer science professor at Princeton) responds to a 2017 talk by Ali Rahimi (an artificial intelligence (AI) researcher) where Rahimi claimed that deep learning/AI learning is now akin to alchemy. Rahimi argued that modern AI was essentially learning through trial and error, and that there were no sound methodologies or theories to assess how those systems were learning.

Broadly, Arora agrees with Rahimi's analysis, and presents a number of examples demonstrating that there are few criteria for choosing one AI architecture over another, few tools to understand how the components of a learned system impact one another, few methods to assess the effectiveness of AI, and so on. Arora does argue, however, that the theories and tools needed to assess AI learning can (and probably will) be developed. The talk is persuasive and is not math-heavy, and I plan to use some of Arora's examples to illustrate points in my paper.

Here is a sample MLA citation and annotation for a paper on the play *God of Carnage*.

The CUNY TV Foundation. *Yasmina Reza's "God of Carnage," with James Gandolfini, Marcia Gay Harden, Jeff Daniels, and Hope Davis.* April 24, 2009, https://is.gd/2fz2hl

This 25-minute interview, sponsored by the CUNY TV Foundation, features James Gandolfini, Marcia Gay Harden, Jeff Daniels, and Hope Davis discussing their 2009 Broadway production of *God of Carnage*. The interview naturally touches on many subjects, but the transplanted context of the play – it was originally written in French – is a recurring theme. The actors have some fascinating insights on how the political context and characters in the play changed out of necessity for an American audience. I have not yet encountered much literature addressing translational issues with the play, and I believe this video could be a key resource if I were to devote a section of my paper to the play's translation.

Here is a sample Chicago citation and annotation for a paper on the selling of body parts.

Koenig, Gaspard. *Do We Really Own Our Bodies?* Online video. TEDxParis, 2016. https://is.gd/KbcwBW

In this 15-minute TED Talk, philosopher Gaspard Koenig argues that French citizens do not have ownership over their own bodies. In France, a popular slogan touts that "my body belongs to me," but Koenig contends that this slogan does not capture the truth of the matter. Activities that French citizens cannot do with their bodies: renting out wombs; selling sex; self-identifying gender; euthanizing themselves; consenting to be eaten; or consenting to being embalmed once dead. Though these are extreme (and weirdly humorous) examples, Koenig notes that human augmentation and ownership of biological data are becoming more prevalent, so legal complications will follow. While Koenig 's examples are taken from French society, his observations have a universal quality, and I will use one or two of his examples in my paper to illustrate the ways in which we lack dominion over our own bodies.

5.11 Government Reports/Technical Reports

Below you will find some tips for annotating government reports and technical reports as well as sample annotations to guide you.

5.11.1 Government Report/Technical Report Annotation Tips

- Because government and technical reports contain informative or explanatory content, they lend themselves well to descriptive and summative annotations.
- Because a typical government or technical report is highly vetted, an evaluative annotation is usually unnecessary beyond noting the trustworthiness of the report.
- You might make an exception to the above, however, when considering reports produced by partisan politicians, undemocratic governments, or profit-driven organizations. These actors have incentives to produce false or misleading information. Evaluating the worth of biased/partisan information is a strategy that always pays off!

5.11.2 Sample Government Report/Technical Report Annotations

Here is a sample APA citation and annotation for a paper on gravitational waves.

The Gravitational Wave International Committee, Shoemaker, D., McLaughlin, M., & Thorpe, J. I. (2019). *Gravitational-wave astronomy in the 2020s and beyond: A view across the gravitational wave spectrum* [Technical Report]. Retrieved from https://is.gd/v1Dy4h

This white paper, sponsored by the National Aeronautics and Space Administration (NASA) and authored by The Gravitational Wave International Committee, is a primer on gravitational waves and their implications for astronomy, cosmology, and astrophysics research through the year 2030. A gravitational wave is a traveling energy wave generated by accelerating large masses. Collapsing stars and colliding black holes, for instance, would produce large gravitational waves.

This is one of the few readable resources I have found about future applications of gravitational waves. Most of the research I found on this topic is either reference material or very specific studies about gravitational waves. Because I am trying to write a paper which could be understood by an undergraduate audience, this source models a writing style I can adopt.

Here is a sample MLA citation and annotation for a paper on Spanish as an official language in the US.

> Congressional Research Service. "English as the Official Language of the United States: Legal Background." *Congressional Research Service*, December 23, 2010, pp. 1–10, https://is.gd/nvrEw4
>
> This report, by the Congressional Research Service, summarizes legislation pertaining to English as an official language in the United States. The report notes that, as of 2010, there is no federal law or constitutional amendment specifying English as the official language of the US. While English may not be an official language in the US, the report notes that both federal and state agencies are legally obliged to provide non-English speakers with certain assistive services. The report concludes by recapping relevant state legislation vis-à-vis English as an official language. The assistive services section of the report is relevant to my paper because I will discuss several legal precedents for providing Spanish speakers with assistive services.

Here is a sample Chicago citation and annotation for a paper on the history of American taxation.

> Internal Revenue Service. "IRS History Timeline." Government Report. Internal Revenue Service, March 2019. https://is.gd/mMDmFx
>
> In this excellent (if selective) history of taxation in the US, the Internal Revenue Service (IRS) highlights 47 American taxation milestones and innovations (occurring between 1765 and 2019). Each is given a slide containing a picture and an explanatory paragraph. As the history of American taxation is incredibly complex, this curated list would be helpful for beginning researchers and popular readers alike.
>
> As one would expect from an IRS document, however, the information is more laudatory than critical. While I appreciate the IRS' triumphalist sense of narrative, I plan to use this source more for reference than for analysis. I might use some of the pictures in my paper, however, as they are terrific!

5.12 Images/Art/Music

Below you will find some tips for annotating images/art/music as well as sample annotations to guide you.

5.12.1 Image/Art/Music Annotation Tips

* If you are annotating a piece of art or music, the most relevant annotation types are descriptive and reflective. If you are an art or music critic, you might find use for evaluative annotations as well.
* If you are annotating an image which is *not* a piece of art (a chart, graph, info-graphic, etc.), it is most likely informative, in which case a summative annotation emphasizing the most salient points of the work is often appropriate.
* For images and art, it makes intuitive sense to append a reduced-size thumbnail image to your annotation, but that is not an accepted practice as of the time of our writing. Ask your instructor if you can include a thumbnail image in your annotated bibliography.

5.12.2 Sample Image/Art/Music Annotations

Here is a sample APA citation and annotation for a paper on women in the Canadian workplace.

Statistics Canada (2017). *History of the Canadian Labour Force Survey, 1945–2016: Chart 2 – Participation rate by sex, 1946–2015* [Online image]. Retrieved from https://is.gd/FVfvVB

This chart, produced by Statistics Canada, shows the participation rate of men and women, and the average participation rate of both sexes, in the Canadian labor force from 1946 to 2015. The trendline for men has declined from approximately 85% participation in 1946 to approximately 70% in 2015; the trendline for women has increased from approximately 25% in 1946 to approximately 60% in 2015. Referring to this chart will bolster my claim that men's participation in the labor force has lowered over time, and at least insofar as this trendline suggests, may continue to marginally decline in the future.

Here is a sample MLA citation and annotation for a paper on grand pianos.

O'Dell, Kailan. "The Evolution of the Grand Piano." *Sono Music,* September 2, 2014, https://is.gd/1uUXHF

This image, produced by Kailan O'Dell and hosted on a webpage sponsored by Sono Music, chronicles the evolution of the grand piano through a series of color drawings. The image features drawings and descriptions of several grand piano variants over the years, including the dulcimer, the clavichord, the spinet, the harpsichord, the square grand piano, the modern grand piano, and others. I plan to use this drawing in my paper, and depending on how my paper shakes out, I might crop it into smaller images to use in different sections (instead of including the unaltered original as an appendix or the like).

Here is a sample Chicago citation and annotation for a paper on Gustave Doré's religious drawings.

Doré, Gustave. "The Tower of Babel." *The Doré Bible Gallery.* 1892. Drawing. https://is.gd/8FetwS

This image, by Gustave Doré, is the sixth plate in the book *The Doré Bible Gallery,* first published in 1892. (The reference I have given here is to the drawing in a digitized version of that book.) The drawing, in black and white, depicts a frenzied collection of worshippers standing before the Tower of Babel. Doré's rendition features a cross-hatched, finely detailed style. I plan to use this image, amongst others, to demonstrate Doré's characteristic style.

5.13 Dissertations

Below you will find some tips for annotating dissertations as well as sample annotations to guide you.

5.13.1 Dissertation Annotation Tips

• You can think of a dissertation as a very long academic article or a book. Given its size, you might want to consider using a combined annotation to capture the essence of the dissertation.

- Dissertations sit on the fine line between emergent scholarship and published works. Given that a dissertation is supposed to contribute new knowledge to a field, it is appropriate to include a significant evaluative annotation.
- Researchers are often interested in only certain parts of a dissertation (typically, the literature review and results sections). If this is the case, simply be upfront about which parts of the dissertation you are annotating.

5.13.2 Sample Dissertation Annotations

Here is a sample APA citation and annotation for a paper on lava–water interaction.

Rawcliffe, H. J. (2015). *Lava–water–sediment interaction: Processes, products and petroleum systems* (doctoral dissertation). University of Glasgow. Retrieved from https://is.gd/ENxnUs

In this doctoral dissertation, Rawcliffe examines the ways in which lava interacts with sediment and water. As per Rawcliffe, "This research identifies a continuum of lava–water–sediment interaction, from minimal and passive interactions, to dynamic and complex interactions, predominantly between basalt lavas and siliciclastic and volcaniclastic sediments" (iii). Rawcliffe suggests her research might best be used by the petroleum industry, who, she notes, are investigating new reservoir systems in search of undiscovered hydrocarbon deposits.

Rawcliffe's fieldwork involved "detailed mapping and logging of siliciclastic, volcaniclastic and volcanic units within four individual field areas" (25). Each field area is given a distinct chapter, and while I found some of the information in the chapters fascinating, I was most interested in Rawcliffe's background/literature review chapter, "Geological Background." This chapter gave me some pertinent material for my own paper, and while parts of the chapter were over my head, I understood the bulk of it and will certainly refer to it throughout my paper.

Here is a sample MLA citation and annotation for a paper on street children in 19th-century literature.

Daniels, Barbara. *Street Children and Philanthropy in the Second Half of the 19th Century.* Doctoral Dissertation, The Open University, 2008, https://is.gd/M7i1cU

This doctoral thesis, by Barbara Daniels, examines mid-19th-century child poverty and the proliferation of children's welfare houses in Britain. Daniels argues that the issue of child poverty came to be a pressing social issue, and in turn, British society (especially politicians, religious groups, and wealthy individuals) took interest in the issue. Crucially, Daniels examines how British attitudes toward the poor rapidly evolved in the latter half of the 19th century, whereas once the poor were viewed as criminals (or criminals-in-waiting), the public came to recognize that many of the poor were actually victims of circumstance. At the time, this shift in thinking was both radical and progressive.

Daniels' thesis is thorough in its coverage, and while she does not touch on literary depictions of 19th-century child poverty, her dissertation gives me a window into how child poverty was perceived by British society.

Here is a sample Chicago citation and annotation for a paper on the prints of William Blake.

Tanaka, Minnie. "The Twelve Large Colour Prints of William Blake: A Study on Techniques, Materials and Context." Nottingham Trent University, 2008. https://is.gd/GZCxMc

This doctoral dissertation, by Minnie Tanaka, examines the color prints made by William Blake in the period 1795–1805. Tanaka attempts a comprehensive analysis, and describes her study as concerned with the "materials, methods, and motives" (p. ii) used by Blade to make the prints. Given the dearth of research I have on the *materials* used by Blake in creating his prints, the two chapters in this thesis that interest me most are "The Development of Blake's Colour Printing Technique" and "Pigments and Method."

By the (appalling) standard of most doctoral writing today, Tanaka's prose was exceptionally clear and direct. The organization of her evidence was also exemplary, and as someone who has only recently begun to study Blake, I followed her thesis without difficulty. Aside from the information in this dissertation, I found Tanaka's Works Cited list helpful, and I have already consulted three of the sources she listed therein.

5.14 Further Reading

5.14.1 Books and Book Chapters

Cave, Roderick, and Sara Ayad. *The History of the Book in 100 Books: The Complete Story, from Egypt to e-Book*. Firefly Books, Inc., 2014.

Eliot, Simon, and Jonathan Rose, editors. *A Companion to the History of the Book*. Blackwell Publishing, 2007.

Houston, Keith. *The Book: A Cover-to-Cover Exploration of the Most Powerful Object of Our Time*. W.W. Norton & Company, 2016.

5.14.2 Journals

Cope, Bill, and Angus Phillips, editors. *The Future of the Academic Journal*. 2nd ed., Chandos Publishing, 2014.

Pyrczak, Fred, and Maria Tcherni-Buzzeo. *Evaluating Research in Academic Journals: A Practical Guide to Realistic Evaluation*. 7th ed., Routledge, 2019.

Regazzi, John J. *Scholarly Communications: A History from Content as King to Content as Kingmaker*. Rowman & Littlefield, 2015.

5.14.3 Magazines

Cox, Howard, and Simon Mowatt. *Revolutions from Grub Street: A History of Magazine Publishing in Britain*. 1st ed., Oxford University Press, 2014.

Gardner, Jared. *The Rise and Fall of Early American Magazine Culture*. University of Illinois Press, 2012.

Sumner, David E. *The Magazine Century: American Magazines Since 1900*. Peter Lang, 2010.

5.14.4 Newspapers

Gooding, Paul. *Historic Newspapers in the Digital Age: "Search All about It!"* Routledge, 2017.

Hansen, Kathleen A., and Nora Paul. *Future-Proofing the News: Preserving the First Draft of History*. Rowman & Littlefield, 2017.

Wallace, Aurora. *Newspapers and the Making of Modern America: A History*. Greenwood Press, 2005.

Williams, Kevin. *Read All about It! A History of the British Newspaper*. Routledge, 2010.

5.14.5 Encyclopedias

Kafker, Frank A., and Jeff Loveland, editors. *The Early Britannica (1768–1803): The Growth of an Outstanding Encyclopedia*. Voltaire Foundation, 2009.

König, Jason, and Greg Woolf, editors. *Encyclopaedism from Antiquity to the Renaissance*. Cambridge University Press, 2013.

Lynch, Jack. *You Could Look It Up: The Reference Shelf from Ancient Babylon to Wikipedia*. Bloomsbury Press, 2016.

5.14.6 Government and Technical Reports

Hering, Heike. *How to Write Technical Reports: Understandable Structure, Good Design, Convincing Presentation*. Springer, 2019.

Lee, Mordecai. *The First Presidential Communications Agency: FDR's Office of Government Reports*. State University of New York Press, 2005.

Riordan, Daniel G. *Technical Report Writing Today*. 10th ed., Wadsworth, 2014.

5.14.7 Videos and Film

Allocca, Kevin. *Videocracy: How YouTube Is Changing the World .. With Double Rainbows, Singing Foxes, and Other Trends We Can't Stop Watching*. Bloomsbury, 2018.

Dixon, Wheeler W., and Gwendolyn Audrey Foster. *A Short History of Film*. 3rd ed., Rutgers University Press, 2018.

Prince, Stephen. *Digital Cinema*. Rutgers University Press, 2019.

5.14.8 Art and Images

Gardner, Helen, and Fred S. Kleiner. *Gardner's Art through the Ages: A Global History*. 16th ed., Cengage Learning, 2020.

Hockney, David, and Martin Gayford. *A History of Pictures: From the Cave to the Computer Screen*. Abrams, 2016.

Wells, Liz, editor. *The Photography Reader: History and Theory*. 2nd ed., Routledge, 2019.

5.14.9 Theses and Dissertations

Bui, Yvonne N. *How to Write a Master's Thesis*. 2nd ed., SAGE, 2014.

Calabrese, Raymond L. *The Dissertation Desk Reference: The Doctoral Student's Manual to Writing the Dissertation*. Rowman & Littlefield Education, 2009.

Lipson, Charles. *How to Write a BA Thesis: A Practical Guide from Your First Ideas to Your Finished Paper*. 2nd ed., The University of Chicago Press, 2018.

5.14.10 Websites and Webpages

Kosseff, Jeff. *The Twenty-Six Words that Created the Internet.* Cornell University Press, 2019.

Nahai, Nathalie. *Webs of Influence: The Psychology of Online Persuasion.* 2nd ed., Pearson Education, 2017.

Lasky, Jack, editor. *The Internet.* Greenhaven Press, 2016.

5.14.11 Blogs and Podcasts

Hendricks, John Allen, and Bruce Mims. *The Radio Station: Broadcasting, Podcasting, and Streaming.* 10th ed., Routledge, 2018.

Leccese, Mark, and Jerry Lanson. *The Elements of Blogging: Expanding the Conversation of Journalism.* Focal Press, 2016.

Spinelli, Martin. *Podcasting: The Audio Media Revolution.* Bloomsbury Academic, 2019.

6

COMPOSING YOUR ANNOTATIONS

6.1 The Context

As you gather sources, use your time well to extract what you need from them. To do this, you will need to take notes, and this can be difficult. In this chapter, we will introduce strategies for getting information from your sources into your annotations. In the first section, you will learn how to write a good descriptive annotation by finding basic information about your source from three places: the source itself, the library (catalog, databases, etc.), and the Internet. In the next section, you will learn how to write your summative annotation by using your source's purpose, organization, and format to guide you. Finally, you will learn how to write your evaluative and reflective annotations by using your notes and the source itself.

6.2 Getting Material into a Descriptive Annotation

When you are researching, one of the first things you might want to do is write a very simplified version of an annotated bibliography, which is known as a **preliminary annotated bibliography**. If you are writing a preliminary annotated bibliography, it might be comprised of only descriptive annotations. Sometimes instructors will assign a preliminary annotated bibliography to ensure you are on the right track with your research.

Whether you are writing a preliminary or complete annotated bibliography, here are three strategies to ease you into the process of writing your descriptive annotations.

6.2.1 Using the Publication Itself to Find Descriptive Information

To describe a source, you need to record information about it, such as its author, format, publisher, and other pertinent information. You can do a lot of this by using the checklist from *Chapter 4: Types of Annotations*. By scanning the source, you may find all you need before you read it in its entirety.

Starting at the beginning of the source and working your way to the end, look for all the elements you can use to describe it. For example, a journal title may appear in a header or footer. As another example, author credentials may be listed before or after the main body of an article, on a credentials page, on a book cover, or in a foreword. Finally, prefaces and other editorial remarks provide hints about a source's intended audience.

If your citation style requires you to cite page numbers, that is easy to do for print sources, and some online sources have them too. For example, many journal articles are in the PDF format, in which case you can probably find page numbers in the header or footer.

When you use webpages, finding descriptive information can be tricky. If you cannot find information such as author, date of publication, and so on, not only will your descriptive annotation be incomplete, but so will your citation. Sometimes it is difficult to even figure out what a webpage's title really is, especially in heavily formatted or very large websites with many sections and pages. You may need to act like a detective to sleuth for clues. If you cannot find what you need, look at the URL: the author, date, or title may be embedded there. Another place to look for descriptive information is the website's homepage or an "About Us" page, where you may find more about the publisher or author.

6.2.2 Using Library Resources to Find Descriptive Information

If you cannot find what you need to describe a source from the source itself, you can always look to your library for help. Library catalogs and databases often provide information about a source, including some or all of the following elements:

- Names of authors and editors
- Publication dates
- Titles of sources, such as article titles and journal titles
- Volume and issue numbers
- Publisher information
- Descriptive features of the source itself
- Source format (e.g., report, book, etc.)
- Names of databases
- **Permalinks** and digital object identifiers (DOIs)

Of course, you can also consult a librarian, who will be more than happy to help you find information about a source.

6.2.3 Search the Internet

If you still need information about a source, perform an Internet search on it. This is especially helpful when you want to know more about the publisher or author of a source. For example, when you are looking for a journal title and all you have are the journal's initials, such as *JAMA,* an Internet search can reveal that *JAMA* is in fact an acronym for *Journal of the American Medical Association.* As another example, you can also search the Internet for information about authors, such as their place of employment, educational credentials, or their first name. An added benefit is that sometimes, by searching for an author, you will find other relevant publications by that same person, some of which might even be better than the one you have.

6.3 Summarize Your Source Efficiently

To read and take notes efficiently for your summative annotations, take a moment to scan your source to find its **rhetorical purpose**. A rhetorical purpose is the main intention of a source: to inform, explain, persuade/argue, or entertain. Also, take note of a source's **organizational mode**. An organizational mode is the underlying logical structure of a text (e.g., comparison–contrast, cause–effect, etc.).

In this section, you will also learn how to use the **source features** to write your summative annotations. By "source features" we mean the parts of a source (e.g., index, glossary, tables, etc.) and the way a source is broken up (e.g., sections, chapters, etc.). Finally, in this section we talk about how to reword your information in order to avoid plagiarism.

6.3.1 Using the Rhetorical Purpose of the Source You Are Summarizing

In applying many of the principles of annotations, deciding on how much of a given source you intend to use depends not only on your own purpose, but also on the rhetorical purpose of your source. These are the four types of rhetorical purposes:

- To inform – sources are meant to relay factual content (as in encyclopedias, dictionaries, and many fact-based webpages)
- To explain – sources are meant to teach concepts (as in many textbooks as well as instructional webpages)
- To persuade/argue – sources are meant to change or bolster opinion, to critique, or to inspire an audience to action (as in most scholarly articles, books, and opinion pieces)
- To entertain – sources are meant to delight or stir emotions (as in literature or other forms of art)

Knowing the rhetorical purpose of a source will help you to write notes efficiently and create a good summative annotation, one that acknowledges that rhetorical purpose. Finally, as you summarize each source, use the summative annotation checklist from *Chapter 4: Types of Annotations* to guide you.

6.3.2 Summarizing Informational Sources

When summarizing informational sources, select and organize the significant facts and other information according to your paper's purpose. If a source has an abundance of facts, avoid listing them all. If your readers wanted to know everything about the source, they could always access it themselves.

For your summative annotation of an informational source, you may want to use the same organizational pattern that the source does. But beware of getting bogged down in detail. For example, just as recipes divide a list of information into ingredients, preparation, and serving suggestions, so too can you divide a list. For example, if you are annotating a list of facts, create groups of similar facts. As another example, you can group related steps to summarize a detailed procedure rather than naming and explaining each and every step.

6.3.3 Summarizing Explanatory Sources

In annotating explanatory texts, select only the key components of the author's explanation and avoid excessive detail. Your purpose is to capture the essence of the author's reasoning, not reproduce the entire source. Rewording explanatory sources can be difficult; for help, see the section on rewording sources, below.

6.3.4 Summarizing Persuasive Sources

To summarize a persuasive text, you will need to briefly tell what the author's position is, as well as what the author is arguing against. In other words, tell what the context of the argument is, as succinctly as possible. Then attempt to reproduce the main line of argument in your own words, also as succinctly as possible.

As you summarize, pay attention to who says what – your source may raise points of disagreement with the author's position. Be careful to distinguish these oppositional points of view from the source's main line of argument. However, the oppositional arguments reported by the author may be of use to you, especially if you are writing an argumentative/persuasive paper or if you want to address the different points of view pertaining to your topic.

6.3.5 Summarizing Entertainment Sources

Your goal in summarizing an entertainment source is to give readers an idea of the whole without going into too much detail: be concise. One mistake novice writers make is to retell a story when all they really ought to do is provide a nutshell summary. For example, in literature, this means reporting essential plot, main characters, setting, themes, and other important components such as symbolism. Stick to what is most relevant to your research.

6.3.6 Summarizing Multi-purpose Sources

Many works have several purposes. In academic writing, you will use sources that are both informational and argumentative. Some works, like satire, are both argumentative and entertaining. And so on.

6.4 Using the Organizational Mode of the Source You Are Summarizing

You may also consider the organizational mode of the source as you take notes. Some of the most common rhetorical modes can be helpful as you take notes because they can guide you in your search for ideas to use in your paper. It is also useful for your notes to reflect the organizational mode of your source. As you scan the source, check for section headings or chapter titles to guide you because headings often reflect the source's organizational mode. Many texts contain elements that combine several modes. Some common organizational modes are explained in Sections 6.4.1–6.4.5.

6.4.1 Comparison–contrast

If the source compares and contrasts ideas, look for differences between the ideas being compared. If the author takes a stand while comparing two things, pay attention to evaluative comments about which thing the author prefers. Comparison–contrast sources have two ways of being organized. In a subject-by-subject comparison, the ideas being compared are discussed separately, usually with a conclusion that ties them together. In a point-by-point comparison, both ideas are discussed together, feature by feature. Again, there usually is a conclusion that brings everything together.

6.4.2 Cause–effect

If your source is largely about causes, look for passages that explain immediate and remote causes, contributory causes, causal chains, and so on. If your source is largely about effects, look for passages that explain short-term and long-term effects, as well as main effects and side effects. Some sources will discuss both causes and effects, so look for everything.

6.4.3 Problem–solution

The problem–solution source may be organized into two parts: a problem analysis and a section on solutions. Using the journalistic questions (*Who?, What?, When?, Where?, Why?,* and *How?*) will be helpful in this work. Look for key components in the problem analysis, such as what/who causes the problem, what/who are most affected, why the problem exists, and where/how the problem occurs. In the solution section, look for the main components of the solution in the same manner. If alternative solutions are suggested, try to establish the optimal one.

6.4.4 Narration

Narrative sources are those that tell a story, either fictional or nonfictional. Above, we explained about summarizing fiction, but to summarize non-fiction, you need a few other tricks. For example, to summarize biographical writing, tell your reader about who is involved, the highlights of the events in question, and the significance of said events. In short, tell your readers only what they need to know to understand the central figures and major events associated with your topic. Be sure, however, to refer to the historical period of the event in order to provide context.

6.4.5 Process

A text that explains a process is about how something is done or how something happens. It proceeds chronologically. It may have steps and it may include a cause–effect component. To summarize a process with many steps, try to chunk some steps together (e.g., a recipe will list ingredients, steps in preparation, and advice about cooking) rather than listing every step in full.

6.5 Using the Features of the Source You Are Summarizing

Source features can help you summarize a work. For example, books are format-ted with chapters and journal articles have sections. Sometimes, chapter or section headings can help you prioritize which content to include in your summative annotation. If you have scanned the entire source, you can then judge how much of it you actually need to read (e.g., maybe you want to use something from a book chapter and not the entire book, so you summarize only the chapter). Use section headings, chapter titles, and other features (such as charts and tables) as guides to help you find the most important information to summarize.

6.5.1 Overview the Format

As an extended example, let us imagine you are going to use an experimental report in your research paper. First look at the report's format. Experimental reports tend to have the same basic format across sources and disciplines, with slight variation. The first part of a research report contains an introduction, a literature review, and the research questions. Some experimental reports include a section justifying the research. Most experimental reports contain informational and explanatory sections to inform readers about materials, data collection methods, source of the data (e.g., subjects or participants), analysis methods, and findings. Finally, they have discussion and/or concluding sections that are persuasive because they interpret findings.

6.5.2 Literature Review or Background Section?

In the literature review section of an experimental report, the author provides necessary background on an issue, and it typically contains citations to other sources. For you, these are secondary sources. Depending on your writing purposes, decide whether to include any of the information from secondary sources in your summary. If the information is not directly concerned with your work, you can safely omit it from your summative annotation. However, if secondary source information is very relevant and you need to include it, be sure to note the secondary author in your annotation so you remain clear about who says what. In this case, you will need to use **indirect quotations** to the authors cited in your original source. Check your documentation manual for help on this matter (e.g., *The Chicago Manual of Style* or *A Pocket Style Manual*).

6.5.3 Methods or Analysis Section?

In your summative annotation, name the methods used to collect data, the type and source of data (e.g., the number and types of participants in a survey), and the type of analysis the authors used to interpret their data. Unless your paper is going to analyze or dispute methodology, you may be able to keep this section brief – perhaps even one sentence. If your paper focuses on questions of methodology, however, go into more depth.

In recent times, some scientific journals have taken to including methods in a footnote rather than the body of a text, in recognition that many readers are reluctant to slog through an indifferently written methods section.

6.5.4 Findings, Discussion, or Conclusion?

Include the major findings of a research study unless your sole focus is on the source's methodology. You may be able to report on the major findings by skimming through the "Findings" section of the report. The conclusions the authors draw may be useful to you, so you can read through the "Discussion" or "Conclusion" sections to find them.

6.5.5 Single Piece of Information?

If you use a source for a single piece of information, you have no need to summarize the entire source. Instead, simply report the information you plan to use. Even if your summative annotation is short, you still should write a brief descriptive annotation of the source, and possibly an evaluative sentence telling why the source (or the piece of information from the source) is credible. Finally, you can include a reflective annotation about how you will use the information in your paper.

6.5.6 Tips for Rewording Successfully

In some cases, paraphrasing (rewording) texts for a summative annotation may be easy (e.g. "the metropolitan area of Chicago and its suburbs" can be "Chicago's greater metropolitan region"). In other cases, you may find difficulty rewording the source text.

As you compose your annotation, if you find yourself looking back and forth from the source to what you are writing, you may end up with too many details – and too many words – in your annotation. You may even end up with too many phrases and quotes from the original source. If this applies to you, try this: read through the source quickly. Then – without looking at the source – summarize what you recall, using your own words. If you use this method, you are more likely to remember the main points than the trivial details. After you have written what you remember, check your work for accuracy, and ensure you have not missed a key point or accidentally plagiarized.

Finally, while you need to pay attention to the way you reword sources, there are times when you do not need to worry very much, especially when you are using common phrases that litter academic writing. For example, do not try to reword things like statistical findings (e.g., $p \leq .001$), population numbers, or the Latin names of animals. In cases like these, you won't have to reword the original source much (or at all). Check with your instructor if you are unsure about paraphrasing.

6.6 Evaluate Your Source Strategically

While the evaluative annotation may not be very long – sometimes a sentence or two will suffice – writing that annotation will take some thought.

To be strategic, write the evaluative annotation in three phases. First, if you are writing a preliminary bibliography with mostly descriptive annotations, you can make a quick note if a source appears to be particularly valuable (or worthless).

Even before you read, you may decide that a source is trustworthy or untrustworthy based on descriptive factors such as whether it was peer-reviewed.

Second, if you decide to use a source, you will most likely write a summative annotation, and as you do, you can write an evaluative annotation. If you decide that the source is not valuable, you can simply make a note of that in your annotation and move on.

Third, you can evaluate your sources after you have read and described and summarized all of them. This is the time you have a firm understanding of the variety and scope of your sources. At that point, you will be able to judge each source in light of the others, and to write or modify your evaluative annotations appropriately.

6.7 Reflect on Your Sources Strategically

There are three times you can write and rewrite your reflective annotations if you want to be efficient. First, whenever you get an idea about how and where to use a source, jot it down. You would be surprised at how easy it is to forget such things when it comes time to write your paper. Second, after you have finished other annotations for your source, write a reflective annotation to record your ideas about how to use that source. Third, after you have annotated all the sources you plan to consult, review your reflective annotations and make additions/changes where necessary.

If you are strategic at this point in your research process, you will be able to use your reflective annotations to help you outline your paper, as you will see in *Chapter 7: Crunch Time – Annotated Bibliography in Process*.

6.8 Further Reading

We introduced many concepts in this chapter. If you would like to know more about them, we suggest you have a look at the following:

Aaron, Jane E., and Ellen Kuhl Repetto. *The Compact Reader: Short Essays by Method and Theme*. 11th ed., Bedford/St. Martins, 2019.

Anker, Susan. *Real Writing with Readings: Paragraphs and Essays for Success in College, Work, and Everyday Life*. 8th ed., Bedford/St. Martins, 2019.

Teufel, Simone, and Marc Moens. "Summarizing Scientific Articles: Experiments with Relevance and Rhetorical Status." *Computational Linguistics*, vol. 28, no. 4, 2002, pp. 409–445.

Works Cited

Hacker, Diana, and Nancy I. Sommers. *A Pocket Style Manual*. 8th ed., Bedford/St Martin's, 2018.

The University of Chicago Press, editor. *The Chicago Manual of Style*. 17th ed., University of Chicago Press, 2017.

7

CRUNCH TIME – ANNOTATED BIBLIOGRAPHY IN PROCESS

7.1 Introduction

Crunch time is here! Your annotated bibliography is complete, and now it is time to write your paper. This chapter explains how to get information from your annotated bibliography into a Works Cited/Bibliography/References list, a **workspace** for planning and writing, an outline, and a rough draft of your research paper.

In this chapter you will find steps for each of the above tasks. You can use one or all of them. Keep in mind that these steps are meant to save you time in your research. After all, the notes you write in an annotated bibliography serve as a sort of external memory. Many an undergraduate senior thesis, a master's thesis, or a doctoral dissertation includes dozens (or even hundreds) of sources. Keeping track of all your research is crucial, and this chapter will help you streamline your process.

7.2 The Context

Often, the annotated bibliography is not the final assignment, but a step toward the final assignment. Sometimes you turn it in before starting your paper (and you may receive instructor comments on it), and other times you turn it in with your paper. Some students consider the annotated bibliography busywork, so they fail to take advantage of the work they put in to create it. They may even make the huge mistake of waiting until after they write their paper to create their annotated bibliography. If you do that, you will indeed be doing busywork, and at the worst possible time – right when your paper is due! Instead of squandering your time, you can learn to use the annotated bibliography in your research-writing process in a way that saves you time and makes writing your paper easier.

By writing your annotated bibliography before you begin writing your paper, you can employ four essential strategies to save time. Use your annotated bibliography to do the following:

- Make a Works Cited/Bibliography/References list
- Make an organized workspace to plan and write
- Create an outline for your research paper
- Create a rough draft of your research paper

7.3 Works Cited/Bibliography/References List

This is a simple step. Make an electronic copy of your annotated bibliography and rename it something else. Then, erase all your annotations, leaving just your citations. Now, it is no longer an *annotated* bibliography, it is a regular bibliography, so retitle your list (e.g., Works Cited, Bibliography, References, etc.). If you used an online tool to generate your annotated bibliography, you can use the same tool to remove the annotations or to generate your new bibliography. (See below for a list of online tools.)

Once your citation list is complete, you will be able to insert or paste this file into your paper. Depending on your research paper format, your list will either follow at the end of your paper or begin on a new page. Most formal papers require it to begin on a new page.

Caution: when using this method, remove any citations you do not use in your paper, and insert any additional citations of sources you have used that were not already listed. Finally, double-check that the citations are alphabetized.

The strategy explained above is very useful, even if you decide to skip the following steps to create an outline, a workspace, and a rough draft. However, if you do the following steps, you can still use your list of citations.

7.4 Annotated Bibliography as Workspace

Even after you turn in your annotated bibliography, you can use it as a workspace, which is a convenient location for keeping your notes organized. Furthermore, you can add useful material to the workspace, such as quotes, in-text citations, and your own commentary and ideas. You can even add new sources and annotations.

There are a few steps for using the annotated bibliography as a workspace, described below, and you will find that it is a valuable way to help you plan and develop your research paper.

7.4.1 Actually Make Your Annotated Bibliography a Workspace!

First, make a copy of your annotated bibliography and rename it whatever you want, such as "Notes." This is an important step because you do not want to lose your completed annotated bibliography!

7.4.2 Review Your Work

The second step is to review what you have, using your annotations to remind you about what you have learned as well as how to use your sources. Look for connections among sources. Jot notes in the workspace if you feel so inclined. Your goal is to get a better mental picture of your final paper.

7.4.3 Add Material

The third step is a matter of adding material to your workspace. This can include material that you did not include in your annotated bibliography but that you plan to use in your paper (such as quotes and paraphrases of key ideas). You may even add charts or graphs. At this stage, be sure to add in-text citations after each key idea you have taken from your sources. Typically, you would do this in the (author page) or (author year page) format.

Finally, add your own ideas. Remember, in your final research paper you will need to comment on and explain the ideas from your sources. Use the workspace to make a quick note of any ideas you get during the review stage.

7.4.4 Omit Material

The fourth and final step is cleaning up your file. Once you are satisfied that you have everything you need for your paper, remove anything you do not need.

First, remove citations of sources you do not plan to use. Then, look over what is left to remove other extraneous material. This will probably include the bulk of your reflective annotations (if you have written any), excessive descriptive information (many research papers do not need to use the titles of works, for example, in the body of the paper), and evaluations of source credibility. However, keep any evaluative commentary that seems like something you could include in your paper, such as positive and negative critiques of the ideas and arguments.

7.5 Annotated Bibliography as Outline

Whether or not your instructor requires you to create an outline for your paper, advanced writers find that a basic outline helps them organize and generate a rough draft.

Create an outline in a new file/document or in your workspace. In your outline, list the main sections of your paper. Then, plug the names of your source authors into the sections of the outline wherever their ideas are relevant.

At this point, remember that a good research paper uses sources synthetically, which means that you combine ideas from several sources. Thus, any given section of your outline may cite several authors. It is also very likely that you will use some of your sources in more than one section. Finally, the outline will help you see where further research is still necessary, as well as places where you can insert your own ideas.

If you want to create a simple outline of just key ideas and authors you will use in each section, your outline might look like the one in Figure 7.1.

    I. Introduction

        A. Context of the issue
        B. Context of the issue
        C. Purpose of your paper
        D. Thesis
        E. Brief statement about the major points to be raised

   II. First section [fill this in with your first specific major point]

        A. Topic 1.1 (authors A, B, F)
        B. Topic 1.2 (authors A, C, D)
        C. Topic 1.3 (author G)

  III. Second section [fill this in with your second specific major point]

        A. Topic 2.1 (authors C, D)
        B. Topic 2.2 (author E)

  IV. Third section

        A. Topic 3.1 (authors E, G, H)
        B. Topic 3.2 (authors A, G, H)
        C. Topic 3.3 [you have an idea for a topic but no source yet]

   V. Fourth section

        A. Topic 4.1 (authors B, F)
        B. Topic 4.2 (authors G, H)
        C. Topic 4.3 (you have an idea for which you do not need a source)

  VI. Conclusion

FIGURE 7.1 Template for Outlining with Topics and Source Authors.

7.6 Annotated Bibliography as Rough Draft

Whether you take steps to create an outline or a Works Cited/Bibliography/References list, you can use your annotated bibliography to create a rough draft of your research paper. In this step, you either use your outline or create headings for the sections of your paper, and then place information from your workspace into the appropriate section headings. If the style of your paper does not call for headings, you may erase the headings once your information is properly ordered.

Here is how to do this: (1) create a new file/document for your paper; (2) insert your outline (if you have one) or create headings in this new file/document; (3) insert everything from your workspace wherever it fits to create an elaborate outline; (4) write topic sentences; and (5) erase any unneeded headings.

Though the first two steps of making a rough draft are straightforward, the third strategy is a bit more complex. To get started on the third step – which is inserting material from your workspace – first look through your workspace. Find ideas that are repeated, closely related, or expanded upon in multiple sources. Some people like to color-code at this stage by using the highlighter function in their word processor. You may need to split up an annotation into several pieces if it has several ideas.

Since you will be moving things around, make sure to put an in-text citation after each unique idea (not necessarily after every sentence) if you have not already done this.

Now, step 3 requires that you cluster your ideas by topic. If you have an outline, you can insert the clustered ideas directly into it. If you have headings, insert the clustered ideas directly under the relevant heading. You may end up with a very elaborate outline of key ideas and some of the content you plan to use in each section. Your resultant outline might look like the one in Figure 7.2.

I. Introduction

    A. Context of the issue

    B. Purpose of your paper

    C. Thesis

    D. Brief statement about the major points to be raised

II. First section [fill this in with your first specific major point]

    A. Topic 1.1 (relevant annotations from authors A, B, F)

    B. Topic 1.2 (relevant annotations from authors A, C, D)

    C. Topic 1.3 (relevant annotations from author G)

III. Second section [fill this in with your second specific major point]

    A. Topic 2.1 (relevant annotations from authors C, D)

    B. Topic 2.2 (relevant annotations from author E)

(Continued)

(Continued)

> IV. Third section
>
>   A. Topic 3.1 (relevant annotations from authors E, G, H)
>
>   B. Topic 3.2 (relevant annotations from authors A, G, H)
>
>   C. Topic 3.3: (you have an idea for a topic but no source yet)
>
> V. Fourth section
>
>   A. Topic 4.1 (relevant annotations from authors B, F)
>
>   B. Topic 4.2 (relevant annotations from authors G, H)
>
>   C. Topic 4.3 (you have an idea for which you do not need a source)
>
> VI. Conclusion

FIGURE 7.2 Template for Elaborate Outline with Topic, Authors, and Annotations.

Turning your elaborately detailed outline into a rough draft is the final strategy in this process. At the beginning of each section of your outline, you will now write a topic sentence to introduce your main points. Then all you need to do is remove the numbering and (possibly) the headings and change the indentation. Voila! You now have a rough draft that might look something like the one in Figure 7.3.

> [Paragraph 1] Introduction's context of the issue. Purpose of your paper. Thesis. Brief statement about the major points to be raised.
>
> [Paragraph 2] Topic sentence for first point. Topic 1.1 (relevant annotations from authors A, B, F).
>
> [Paragraph 3] Topic 1.2 (relevant annotations from authors A, C, D).
>
> [Paragraph 4] Topic 1.3 (relevant annotations from author G).
>
> [Paragraph 5] Topic sentence for second point. Topic 2.1 (relevant annotations from authors C, D).
>
> [Paragraph 6] Topic 2.2 (relevant annotations from author E).
>
> [Paragraph 7] Topic sentence for third point. Topic 3.1 (relevant annotations from authors E, G, H).
>
> [Paragraph 8] Topic 3.2 (relevant annotations from authors A, G, H).
>
> [Paragraph 9] Topic 3.3 (you have an idea for a topic but no source yet).
>
> [Paragraph 10] Topic sentence for fourth point. Topic 4.1 (relevant annotations from authors B, F).
>
> [Paragraph 11] Topic 4.2 (relevant annotations from authors G, H).
>
> [Paragraph 12] Topic 4.3 (you have an idea for which you do not need a source).
>
> [Paragraph 13+] Conclusion.

FIGURE 7.3 Template for Rough Draft.

7.7 Final Words

If you have done one or more of the steps explained in this chapter, you have made significant progress in your writing. If you have a rough draft, you are ready to write your research paper in a more polished manner. Congratulations!

In *Chapter 8: Tools and Strategies for Working Online*, you will find some methods for writing an annotated bibliography with a group of research partners. You will also find lists of online tools to help you generate citations and annotations, and ideas about using online tools to publish your annotated bibliography.

7.8 Further Reading

We introduced many concepts in this chapter, and if you would like to know more about them, we suggest you have a look at the following:

Fitzpatrick, Damian, and Tracey Costley. "Using Annotated Bibliographies to Develop Student Writing in Social Sciences." *Discipline-Specific Writing: Theory into Practice*, edited by John Flowerdew and Tracey Costley, Routledge, 2017, pp. 113–125.

8

TOOLS AND STRATEGIES FOR WORKING ONLINE

This chapter describes tips on the use of online platforms to help create citations and annotated bibliographies; strategies for creating and using annotated bibliographies in collaborative settings using online tools; and information about publishing annotated bibliographies in print and online.

8.1 Creating Annotated Bibliographies and Citations with Online Tools

You can create citations (and endnotes and footnotes) in Microsoft Word or Google Docs in the American Psychological Association (APA), Modern Language Association (MLA), and Chicago styles. Unfortunately, there are no annotated bibliography generators in Microsoft Word or Google Docs. However, there are many other tools you can use.

The following list of online tools for generating bibliographies eases the process of compiling an annotated bibliography. This list is ever-changing, and we have included only the most popular services used by our students. If you use an online tool, ensure that it outputs citations in the documentation style you need.

Here are some of the more common online citation-building tools:

- BibMe (www.bibme.org/#)
- Citation Machine (www.citationmachine.net/)
- Cite This For Me (www.citethisforme.com/)
- CiteFast (www.citefast.com/)
- Zotero (www.zotero.org/)

8.2 The Use of Annotated Bibliographies in Collaborative Research

Much research is conducted collaboratively, such as in group projects. For many research teams, that collaboration occurs online. Microsoft Word Online and Google Docs have greatly eased the process of writing together online. If you are working on a group project, consider using the services listed above to generate your citations and annotated bibliography. However, there are also useful strategies and other apps that facilitate collaborative research. These are explained below.

8.2.1 Strategy 1: Share a Document

One way to collaborate on your annotated bibliography is to make a shared document, such as a Google Doc, in which you and your research partners enter citations, organize them, and create annotations. By working collaboratively, you and your research partners will avoid duplicating work, benefit by reading one another's annotations, and enable one another to add comments, such as "Let's use this source."

8.2.2 Strategy 2: Create a Shared Database

Another method for collaboration in research writing is to create a shared database, such as an Excel Workbook or a Google Sheet. This is a simple and flexible strategy. Create a spreadsheet in Excel or Google Sheets. In one column, enter the citations. Then, in one or more columns, enter annotations. Some people like to create a column for each type of annotation. Cindy and one of her research partners have used a method whereby they created one column for citations, a second column for descriptive and summative annotations, and a third column for evaluative and reflective annotations. It was easy to keep the citations alphabetized, and easy for the entire team to enter citations and annotations.

Once your annotated bibliography is complete in the spreadsheet, it is easy to turn it into a document that you can insert into your paper. That is what Cindy and her research partner did, in fact. They made a rough set of headings at the beginning of their shared document in the space where their paper would go; then they put the annotated bibliography at the bottom of their document. As they wrote their paper, whenever they used a source, they removed the annotation (and left the citation) until all they had left was a References list.

8.2.3 Strategy 3: Use Software to Compose and Collaborate

Some people like to use software to plan, organize, and write research papers. Writers find that software tools help them remain organized as they work, and some allow writers to collaborate easily. Here are the most commonly used research tools, some of which have collaborative features built in:

- Diigo Web Collector (www.diigo.com/): Diigo has a Chrome extension that allows users to collect, organize, annotate, and share webpages and PDFs.
- EndNote (https://endnote.com/product-details/basic/): EndNote provides a free basic version, available only online. It helps writers organize and cite sources in twenty-one citation styles. It also features a "Cite While You Write" feature which inserts references and automatically formats citations while you write your papers in Word.
- Evernote (https://evernote.com/): Evernote is useful for managing time in large projects, but it has a note-taking space that allows writers to create a sort of annotated bibliography. The notes section will accommodate each source.
- Mendeley (www.mendeley.com): Mendeley has many functions, among which it allows writers a space to keep a library, to highlight text, and to take notes. One of its extensions allows users to add text files from a desktop as well as source texts found on the Internet. Mendeley also has a Chrome extension for citing sources, which is most useful for citing webpages.
- NoodleTools (www.noodletools.com/): NoodleTools has a free version that helps writers organize, cite sources, and create outlines.
- Omeka (www.omeka.net/): Omeka is a publishing platform used to curate a webpage for a set of artifacts (texts and images) in an organized manner. It allows users to create and attach descriptive tags to each artifact, including tags for different types of annotations. The resulting webpage is an exhibit that, while not an annotated bibliography *per se*, performs much the same functions.
- PowerNotes (powernotes.com): PowerNotes can be used flexibly, and anyone can use it for one project without charge, making it a good choice for those working on a big project.
- Scrivener (www.literatureandlatte.com/): Scrivener helps you write your annotations, reference citations, and research paper. A nice feature is that it allows you to view your material in multiple ways, so you can easily split, reorder, and combine notes. It comes with a free trial.
- Zotero (www.zotero.org/): Zotero is an open-source software and is free to everyone. Zotero allows you to collect and cite your research, keep it organized, and share it with others. It can link to other programs and has a Chrome extension.

Many more tools are available for creating and sharing annotated bibliographies in collaborative settings. Wikipedia keeps a list, frequently updated, of free tools that writers and researchers can use ("Comparison of Reference Management Software").

8.3 Annotated Bibliography for Publication

Remember, some annotated bibliographies are not only part of a research-writing process, but are also publishable in their own right. Annotated bibliographies are published in various formats: books and technical reports, academic journals, and online forums. Whereas some annotated bibliographies appear as a webpage on professional organizations' websites, others are gathered elsewhere online. They serve as collections helpful to disciplinary researchers.

The published annotated bibliography has a long tradition in disciplines such as history, education, library science, communication and rhetoric, literature, and writing studies. It appears to be gaining popularity in other areas as well, such as psychology, sociology, and business. While not unheard of in the sciences, they are less common in the physical and biological sciences than in the humanities, arts, and social sciences.

One close relative of the annotated bibliography is the bibliographic essay, especially in the humanities. Typically, a bibliographic essay's citations and annotations are organized first thematically, and then by publication date or author. What distinguishes the bibliographic essay from an annotated bibliography is the addition of running commentary throughout the essay, so that it reads almost like a traditional essay. If this sort of writing interests you, scan professional journals and publishers in your field to see whether they publish bibliographic essays.

Another close relative of the annotated bibliography, online archival collections, is becoming popular in the digital humanities. Online archives collect resources/artifacts (texts and images) that are displayed and accessible on websites. Digital archives are typically collections of items that do not otherwise have a presence on the Internet (e.g., artworks, scanned texts, and objects such as antique furniture or coins) so that others can search, analyze, and use the artifacts. Platforms such as Drupal and Omeka are two of the most popular content management systems in the digital humanities (Dombrowski 290–292). They allow users to add descriptive information to the items in their own collection, including annotative paragraphs.

As resources have become more widely accessible, so too have annotated bibliographies, many of which are published online. It strikes us that the online annotated bibliography is an ideal way for students to share the fruits of their labor after they have done an exhaustive literature search. Approaching an editor with an idea for your annotated bibliography may be the first step in a long list of publications to your credit.

8.3.1 Parts of a Published Annotated Bibliography

When you write an annotated bibliography for others, consider your audience's needs and the specific professional context of your work. If seeking to publish, you should ensure your annotated bibliography has an introduction, an organized list of annotations, and probably concluding remarks of some sort.

The Introduction

In your introduction, provide an overview of the topic area, and explain the purpose and scope of your project, and your **organizational principle** (if warranted). Your organizational principle is the reason you order your entries the way you do (e.g., alphabetically or chronologically).

The Organized List of Annotation Entries

While most annotated bibliographies are organized alphabetically, the organizational principle you use should suit your purposes and the material being annotated. You have many options, such as the following:

- Alphabetical
- Chronological (date of publication or period of subject matter, e.g., decade, century, etc.)
- Topical (e.g., your main topic divided into sensible and largely discrete and meaningful areas)
- Source format (e.g., articles, books, DVDs, government documents, films, artworks, and webpages, etc.)
- Language and translations (especially good for annotated bibliographies of literature)
- Location (e.g., grouped by country of origin or the location of the sources themselves, such as for museum collections, art, and music)
- Methodological
- Any orderly combination of the above you see fit to use

8.3.2 Annotation Types in Published Annotated Bibliographies

Because the published annotated bibliography is geared toward specific readers, consider your audience and purpose as you write. Be conscious of your readers' needs and prior knowledge. For example, if your annotated bibliography is aimed at sixth-grade teachers, and your sources are all from peer-reviewed education journals or books written for sixth graders, you need not repeat that information in every entry, but simply provide it in an introductory paragraph.

Descriptive Annotations in Published Annotated Bibliographies

Readers of annotated bibliographies are probably very interested in the format and accessibility of your sources. Readers can use your citations to find your sources, and they may want more detailed information before investing additional time. For example, an annotated bibliography of resources for teaching second-grade geography should include descriptive information about the readability level of materials, the inclusion of illustrations and classroom activities, and so on.

Summative Annotations in Published Annotated Bibliographies

When publishing for others, you may need to summarize an entire source, not merely the parts you find interesting. Your goal is typically to overview the source's purpose and arguments so that your readers can decide whether to read the original source. In some cases, though, you can concentrate on summarizing only the highly relevant parts of a source, given the focus and scope of your annotated bibliography. For example, perhaps you are in sociology and your purpose in writing an annotated bibliography is to provide a digest of *only* the findings of empirical research studies on a given topic. In this case, you might include *only* the most concise descriptions of your sources and a one-sentence summary of the methods used, concentrating instead on summarizing the research findings. In another annotated bibliography, you might concentrate on summarizing *only* the research methods of the studies.

Evaluative Annotations in Published Annotated Bibliographies

The evaluative annotation is the place to praise or condemn a source for the benefit of your readers. Your perspective must be wider than if your sole audience were an instructor. You need to anticipate your audience's potential needs because they are probably going to read your annotations in order to facilitate their own work. For example, in an annotated bibliography on a historical topic, you might focus on evaluating the historiographic methods of the sources. In this way, writing evaluative annotations becomes a creative, critical, and time-saving gesture for your readers.

Reflective Annotations in Published Annotated Bibliographies

In writing a reflective annotation for your readers, you are now reflecting on how your audience, not only you, might use a source. For example, an annotated bibliography about adolescent literature, in which you have described a set of works according to their grade-level readability, already implies that the sources might be useful for teachers at those grade levels. But you might also reflect on specific themes in the sources that would be useful to teachers making lesson plans.

Combined Annotations in Published Annotated Bibliographies

Most of the annotations you will write in a published annotated bibliography will be combined, and there is no set rule for which of the other four annotation types you will combine. Your decision should rest on your anticipation of the audience's needs as well as the scope and purpose of your annotated bibliography.

8.4 Further Reading

The use of annotated bibliographies in various disciplines, especially in online and collaborative research projects, is a rapidly changing area. So too are the online tools you can use. If you would like to know more about them, we suggest you have a look at the following:

Bell, Emily. "Research Guides: Citation and Research Management Tools at Harvard: Comparing Citation Tools." *Harvard University*, December 4, 2019, https://is.gd/ZhLSbn

El Khatib, Randa, et al. "Open Social Scholarship Annotated Bibliography." *KULA: Knowledge Creation, Dissemination, and Preservation Studies*, vol. 3, no. 1, 2019, article 24, pp. 1–141, https://is.gd/CXcocY

Gerstein Science Information Centre. "Research Guides: Citation Management: Comparison Table." *University of Toronto Libraries*, January 23, 2019, https://is.gd/jzZAa6

Works Cited

Dombrowksi, Quinn. "Drupal and Other Content Management Systems." *Doing Digital Humanities: Practice, Training, Research*, edited by Constance Crompton et al., Routledge, 2016, pp. 289–302.

Wikimedia Foundation. "Comparison of Reference Management Software." *Wikipedia*, 13 Nov. 2019, https://is.gd/C5st5N

9

SAMPLE ANNOTATED BIBLIOGRAPHIES

9.1 Sample APA Annotated Bibliography

I am writing a research paper about math anxiety and dyscalculia. I do not have a working thesis yet, but I have found many sources about math anxiety and will develop a thesis shortly. I will certainly include material in my paper about strategies for combatting math anxiety.

Ashcraft, M. H. (2019). Models of math anxiety. In I. C. Mammarella, S. Caviola, & A. Dowker (Eds.), *Mathematics anxiety: What is known and what is still to be understood* (pp. 1–19). New York: Routledge.

> This book chapter, by Ashcraft, provides research-based summaries of the predominant models used to describe math anxiety. This chapter provides excellent material to ground my research, and while I have not yet decided which theory/model of math anxiety I find most convincing, I will devote an initial section of my paper to recapping the models Ashcraft identifies.
>
> The models Ashcraft summarizes are the personality construct model (math anxiety derives from aspects of an individual's personality); the cognitive construct model (math anxiety itself is thought to occupy space in an individual's working memory); the sociocultural construct model (teachers, parents, curricula, etc. are thought to influence math anxiety); the gender model (math anxiety is somewhat determined by sex/gender characteristics); the neuro-biological model (math anxiety is somewhat determined by genetic factors); and the interpretation model (an individual's *perception* of why they struggle with math).

Association for Psychological Science. (November 4, 2015). Math anxiety doesn't equal poor math performance. Retrieved September 21, 2019, from https://is.gd/AXzyzO

> This article discusses a study in which the authors examined the relationships between math anxiety, math performance, and math motivation in American college students. The findings of the study were surprising: those with modest math anxiety and high math motivation saw an *increase* in their math performance over time; conversely, those with a degree of math anxiety and a low level of math motivation saw a decrease in their math performance.
>
> This research is significant in that it suggests that interventions to reduce math anxiety may not always be productive and/or advisable. To date in my research, this is the only source I have that points out a "positive" side to math anxiety, and so this source will be valuable. If I end up arguing for specific interventions to reduce math anxiety in my paper, I will refer to this source in discussing the potential costs of said intervention.

Beilock, S. L., & Willingham, D. T. (2014). Math anxiety: Can teachers help students reduce it? *American Educator, 38*(2), 28–32. Retrieved from https://is.gd/1nZQwH

> This article, by Beilock and Willingham, gives teachers an overview of math anxiety and some practical strategies for combatting it. The article provides a selective literature review, addressing issues such as when math anxiety first emerges, which students will be most anxiety-prone, and what social cultural factors contribute to math anxiety. Following that, the article suggests several strategies teachers might use to help fight math anxiety in their classrooms. The article is efficient and well written, packing an enormous amount of information into five pages. The classroom advice is practical, and I plan to discuss some of this advice in my paper.

Chinn, S. J. (2012). *The trouble with maths: A practical guide to helping learners with numeracy difficulties* (2nd ed.). New York: Routledge.

> This book, by Chinn, contains ten chapters on various aspects of dyscalculia (the inability to perform basic math operations) and math learning difficulties. The chapters I plan to use in my research are the following: "Introduction: Learning Difficulties in Maths and Dyscalculia"; "Factors That Affect Learning"; "The Vocabulary and Language of Maths"; and

"Manipulatives and Materials: Multisensory Learning." There is also a math department policy in Appendix #4 that I plan to refer to in my paper.

As the title suggests, this book is aimed at practitioners, and the research and the advice make sense. Furthermore, as some of the dyscalculia research I have run across is very dense, I appreciate Chinn's straightforward style. This book also draws widely from the British educational context, and given that most of my research is from American authors, I think the chapters I use will add dimension to my paper. I also like that this book contains practical examples to illustrate aspects of dyscalculia, and I plan to refer to many of these examples in my paper.

Coles, T. (April 21, 2017). How teens can fight math anxiety. *Bright Magazine*. Retrieved from https://is.gd/LxsP4f

Coles' article chronicles the expansion of mindfulness training in schools and tutoring centers. Coles quotes Randye Semple, a clinical psychologist, who describes "mindfulness" thusly: "Mindfulness means paying attention with intention, non-judgement, and acceptance to what's happening in the present moment" (para. 12). Coles says the success of mindfulness programs in academia has been resounding, and the students who received mindfulness training at the Math Guru tutoring center reported increased confidence and higher performance on math tests. This is the first piece of literature I found that discusses mindfulness training and math anxiety, and the results of the program seem encouraging. I will discuss this research in my paper even though it is from a magazine and does not contain original research.

Doedens-Plant, A. C. R. (2018). *An investigation into the associations between maths anxiety in secondary school pupils and teachers' and parents' implicit theories of intelligence and failure* (Doctoral Dissertation, University of Southampton). Retrieved from https://is.gd/ihm1mp

This doctoral dissertation, by Doedens-Plant, "examined the role that teachers' mindsets, or implicit beliefs about intelligence and failure, play in the development of their pupils' mindsets and subsequent maths anxiety" (p. "abstract"). An empirical study surveyed 859 secondary-school students, 84 parents, and nine teachers in Britain on their beliefs about intelligence and failure in relation to math anxiety. The results make intuitive sense: both students' and teachers' failure beliefs impacted students' math anxiety. The study concludes that math teachers can help reduce math anxiety by ensuring their practice promotes failure as a helpful part of learning. Insofar as I could determine, the study's methodology was sound, and the author's conclusions follow from their evidence.

Dowker, A., & Morris, P. (2017). Targeted interventions for children with difficulties in learning mathematics. In S. Chinn (Ed.), *The Routledge international handbook of dyscalculia and mathematical learning difficulties* (pp. 256–264). New York, NY.

> This short book chapter, by Dowker and Morris, reports on a math intervention program called *Catch Up Numeracy*, which has been used since 2007 with over 45,000 elementary school children in the UK. The program has produced good results, and compared with many other individualized intervention programs, *Catch Up Numeracy* is cost-effective. I was most taken with the "Intensive Interventions" section that reports on the efficacy and costliness of highly individualized intervention programs. The authors suggest, that while these programs may be effective, they could not be rolled out on a mass scale due to their high cost. I will devote a section of my paper to discussing individualized interventions for those suffering from extreme math anxiety/dyscalculia.

Klass, P. (April 24, 2017). Fending off math anxiety. *The New York Times*, p. 4. Retrieved from https://is.gd/gkiSfu

> In this newspaper article, Perri Klass (a medical doctor) recaps some of the current thinking on math anxiety. An area of emphasis throughout the article is the adult/teacher/parent's role in promoting math anxiety. Klass notes that, while many parents are diligent in preparing their children to read, in contrast, they are not as concerned about promoting their children's numeracy. This literacy-over-math bias struck me as important and speaks to my own experience growing up. I have not yet encountered a source discussing this dynamic, and so this article will be useful.

Kranzler, J. H. (2018). *Statistics for the terrified* (6th ed.). New York: Rowman & Littlefield.

> This book, by Kranzler, addresses math anxieties that accompany statistical learning. Statistics are obviously a subset of mathematics, and I would like to devote a section of my paper to statistical learning difficulties. Though I will cite information from the entire book, the three chapters in Section #1 are the most useful for me: "Effective Strategies for Studying Statistics"; "Overcoming Math Anxiety"; and "Basic Math Concepts." In these chapters, Kranzler proposes that rational emotive therapy (a type of psychotherapy) could be used to help overcome math anxieties. Rational emotive therapy aims to overcome emotions that (a) are unpleasant, and (b) lead to self-defeating behaviors. I have not seen this therapy discussed in my other research, but it struck me as quite useful. I plan to discuss how rational emotive therapy could be used to overcome statistical and math anxieties in my paper.

Moreno-García, E., García-Santillán, A., Molchanova, V. S., & Plata Campero, E. (2018). Among the mathematics tasks, math courses and math exams: How's the level of student anxiety toward maths in a private high school in Mexico? *European Journal of Contemporary Education, 7* (4), 741–753. Retrieved from https://is.gd/c1XGq8

> In this study, the authors propose a four-factor model of mathematics anxiety (as derived from a survey of 183 secondary students from private schools in Mexico). The four factors the authors propose are as follows: (1) anxiety when preparing for a math test; (2) anxiety in solving math problems; (3) anxiety about reading mathematics books; and (4) anxiety while taking a math test. I had initially hoped this article would provide me with new information about math anxiety, but it is so incompetently written that it is essentially worthless. I can only assume the authors are the victims of a bad translation. I will not be using this article in my paper.

Nisbet, J. (March 8, 2019). Overcoming math anxiety: 12 evidence-based tips that work. Retrieved September 21, 2019, from https://is.gd/tUBlVg

> This blog entry, by Nisbet, gives teachers and parents a brief overview of math anxiety and tactics for overcoming it. The blog contains four sections about math anxiety: (1) a definition; (2) psychological effects; (3) causes; and (4) 12 tips for overcoming math anxiety. Each section offers a fulsome discussion, and the section containing the 12 tips includes a few strategies for overcoming math anxiety that were new to me. One of the tips, however, recommends that children use the *Prodigy* math learning app, and the *Prodigy* app sponsors this very blog! A disclosure statement would have been nice, but this blog nonetheless contains applicable (if somewhat biased) information, and I hope to use it in my paper.

Shaffer, L. (2015). The fear of math: Five strategies to help students conquer their math anxiety. *Scholastic Instructor, 124*(5), 27–29.

> This magazine article, by Shaffer, reviews five strategies used by elementary school teachers to reduce math anxiety. These are: (1) to promote a growth mindset; (2) to begin each lesson with a comforting warm-up activity; (3) to allow multiple pathways to an answer; (4) to not let speed become a roadblock (when students become demoralized or stuck on a problem); and (5) to make math a game. Though the evidence backing these strategies is anecdotal, I like that the strategies clearly address a common problem in elementary school math. Most of these strategies also incorporate a social/partnering dimension, which a lot of other sources recommend for combatting math anxiety.

Stephens, M., Tang, J. H., Perkins, R., Landeros, K., & Malley, L. (2016). *Highlights from TIMSS and TIMSS advanced 2015: Mathematics and science achievement of U.S. students in grades 4 and 8 and in advanced courses at the end of high school in an international context.* (Government Report No. NCES 2017–002). Retrieved from https://is.gd/rDiPR6

> The Trends in International Mathematics and Science Study (TIMSS) is a study conducted every four years "that measure[s] students' knowledge and skills in mathematics and science and their ability to apply their knowledge in problem-solving situations" (p. 2). The study is conducted with fourth- and eighth-graders, and in 2015 over 50 countries participated. I hoped to use this report to highlight differences in math pedagogy between the US and other countries, and then to triangulate those results with international data on math anxiety. As it turns out, though, the data in this report does not discuss math pedagogy. I might still use some of the data in an introductory and/or background section of my paper. Time will tell.

The Understood Team (2019). *Signs of math anxiety/Signs of dyscalculia* [Online image]. Retrieved from https://is.gd/EK3rqM

> This image, assembled by The Understood Team (a network of non-profits devoted to helping students with learning and thinking difficulties), highlights the differences between math anxiety and dyscalculia. Math anxiety is a form of anxiety that can inhibit math learning or performance, while dyscalculia is a condition which renders one unable to perform math operations in the first instance. The chart is succinct and accurate. I plan to include it in my paper without alteration.

Tobias, S., & Haag, S. (2012). Math anxiety and gender. In J. A. Banks (Ed.), *Encyclopedia of Diversity in Education* (pp. 1441–1444). Thousand Oaks, California: SAGE Publications, Inc.

> This encyclopedia article, by Tobias and Haag, succinctly reviews math anxiety and gender research from 1970 to the present. According to this article, gender differences and math anxiety were first seriously studied in the 1970s, and the main research conclusions of those years were that cultural practices, sex role norms, and differences in male/female brain structures accounted for differences in math anxiety. In the 1980s and 1990s, some research focused on the reasons why girls underperformed at spatial problems. In the post-Millennial period, when controlling for biases and cultural factors, studies reveal few significant differences in math anxiety between men and women. Researchers speculate that cultural norms and pedagogical practices are continuing to reinforce the stereotype that boys are better than girls at math.

Vishton, P. M. (2014). *Getting a jump on math – Without math anxiety* [Video file]. Retrieved from https://is.gd/swb0Uj

> This video discusses three essential strategies to help children succeed in math: (1) ensuring children develop a "number sense" (an intuition of how numbers work and what you can do with them); (2) employing manipulatives in teaching; and (3) promoting a basic understanding of fractions by age ten. The video is research-based and suggests practical strategies that a parent or teacher can use. Although the video was aesthetically bland – it was literally a half-hour of a man standing around talking into the camera with some superimposed graphics – the proposed strategies were new to me, and I will discuss number sense and "fractions-by-age-ten" in my paper.

Young, J. R., & Young, J. L. (2016). Young, black, and anxious: Describing the black student mathematics anxiety research using confidence intervals. *Journal of Urban Mathematics Education*, 9(1), 79–93. Retrieved from https://is.gd/5M30Ir

> This meta-analysis, by Young and Young, aims to "conduct a single group summary of studies using the [Math Anxiety Reporting Scale] to characterize and delineate the measurement of reported [math anxiety] within the Black Student population" (p. 83). In their meta-analysis, the authors analyze 21 studies of K-12 populations that included black students. Regrettably, they could not find enough evidence about black students and math anxiety to draw firm conclusions. The authors' lack of findings suggests an urgent need for more studies devoted to understanding the problems black students have with math anxiety.

9.2 Sample MLA Annotated Bibliography

I am writing a research paper about comic books and graphic novels being treated as literature. I do not have a working thesis yet, but I have found many sources on comic books/graphic novels and literature. There seem to be a few graphic novels which persistently pop up in discussion about comics and literature (as examples, *Maus*, *Watchmen*, *The Dark Knight*), and I will certainly discuss them in my paper.

Chute, Hillary L. "Comics for Grown-Ups?" *Why Comics? From Underground to Everywhere*, Harper, 2017, pp. 1–32.

> This book chapter, by Hillary Chute, discusses the history, evolution, and artistic philosophies of comics written for adults. Chute begins the chapter by explaining why the *medium* of comics is so often conflated with the *genre* of superheroes. She then traces the legacy of non-superhero genres from the

turn of the 20th century to the present. Throughout her history, Chute lays out the differences between "comic strips," "comic books," and "graphic novels," and she spends considerable time analyzing definitional wrinkles of the last term (Chute describes the graphic novel as "expressive, long-form narrative comics" 19). This history will contextualize my paper, and the discussion of graphic novels will help me argue that they share DNA with narrative prose.

Cleaver, Samantha. "Comics & Graphic Novels." *Instructor*, vol. 117, no. 6, 2008, pp. 28–34, https://is.gd/Y2zeOM

This short article, by Samantha Cleaver, highlights pedagogical reasons why comic books and graphic novels are being taught in elementary classrooms. In addition to readily connecting with students, comics help strengthen students' visual and multimodal literacies. Though the article is brief, it reinforces the fact that comics and graphic novels are now taught alongside conventional children's literature. Using this article (and others), I intend to make a populist argument that, as elementary students matriculate, they will bring their assumptions about the literary value of comics with them. We will soon see a change in the popular perception of comics' literary value.

Dale, Andrew. *Graphic Novels: Essential literary genres.* Abdo Publishing, 2017.

Andrew Dale's book contains nine chapters that analyze five graphic novels. The first chapter also introduces the concept of literary genres and discusses approaches to literary analysis. The graphic novels analyzed in the book are *Descender: Tin Stars*; *Lumberjanes: Beware the Kitten Holy*; *Persepolis*; *Maus: A Survivor's Tale Part 1: My Father Bleeds History*; and *March: Book 1*. The first chapter and the chapters analyzing *Maus* will be especially useful to me. The first chapter is helpful in discussing literary genres in a straightforward manner (many other sources are not). Additionally, I can draw from the analysis of *Maus* to inform my own take on the graphic novel. Dale discusses several theoretical lenses (critical race theory, feminist theory, etc.) which I can apply to my analysis of graphic novels as literature.

Emina, Seb. "In France, Comic Books Are Serious Business." *The New York Times*, January 29, 2019, https://is.gd/KKGEUd

This newspaper article, by Seb Emina, reports on the annual Angoulême International Comics Festival, held in France. The article notes that, by sales volume, comics and graphic novels in the French/Belgian market are selling better than they ever have. Those quoted in the article also suggest that the quality of these publications is higher than ever. This scene is contrasted with the American market, where comic book and graphic novel sales are tapering off (as of 2018). Some information from this article will be useful as background/context material for my paper.

Gall, Elisa, and Patrick Gall. "Comics Are Picture Books: A (Graphic) Novel Idea." *Horn Book Magazine*, vol. 91, no. 6, Dec. 2015, pp. 45–50.

In this short magazine article, by Elisa Gall and Patrick Gall, the authors argue that comic books and graphic novels are a subset of picture books. The authors chose to write on this issue because, at the time, the American Library Association was debating whether comics should be eligible for the Caldecott Medal (an award reserved for children's picture books). The authors address how the paneled layouts and visual text features of comics are congruous with the visual grammar of children's picture books. The authors argue that, if you accept that picture books are considered literature, then comics should be considered literature as well. I will use such an argument in my paper.

Hutton, Robert. *Comics and Literature: A Love Story*. Carleton University, 2017, https://is.gd/dNw6CO

As per Hutton, this doctoral dissertation,

> [aims to] suggest that alternative comics authors' relationship to literature has been every bit as torrid and mercurial as any love affair … I hope to shed light on the material conditions and authorial manoeuvres that made the "literary comic" possible.
>
> *(35)*

Though Hutton's prose is turgid, I think he is getting at the idea that alternative comics since the 1960s have incorporated literary tropes in their work. He argues that these efforts have gradually moved the comics industry "diagonally upwards and to the right, obtaining both more freedom and more respect" (32).

Though I would not describe Hutton's work as especially transparent, there are a variety of informational nuggets throughout the dissertation that could bolster the background sections of my own paper. For instance, he has a great discussion about why it was important to comics creators in the 1980s to get their work into traditional bookstores, as the bookstore was then the signifier of literary ambition and freedom.

Jennings, Kimberly Ann, et al. "Fifth Graders' Enjoyment, Interest, and Comprehension of Graphic Novels Compared to Heavily-Illustrated and Traditional Novels." *International Electronic Journal of Elementary Education*, vol. 6, no. 2, 2014, pp. 257–274, https://is.gd/Z0cMqt

This study reports on an experiment wherein 24 fifth-grade students read graphic novels, highly illustrated novels, and regular prose novels. The researchers compared the effectiveness of the three forms in the teaching of reading. Though there were few participants in this study, the authors conclude that the graphic novels were the most effective of the three formats at promoting reading comprehension and discussion, and they recommend continued use of graphic novels in the K-6 reading classroom.

Though this study does not directly address my research question ("are comics literature?"), I selected this article because it foregrounds some of the literary similarities between graphic novels, illustrated novels, and prose novels. Also, I would like to make the argument in my paper that, as graphic novels continue to be used in elementary classrooms, they will increasingly be normalized as literature. This article will also help me make the case that comics and graphic novels will continue to find their way into elementary school classrooms.

Kellett, Dave, and Frederick Schroeder. *Stripped*. Sequential Films, 2014, https://is.gd/HVmMom

This documentary film, by Dave Kellett and Frederick Schroeder, gives voice to several prominent cartoonists as they discuss the artistry, cultural impact, and business of comic strips. Aside from being a great background resource, the film also touches on the ways that newspaper-specific pressures (e.g., the pressure to produce daily content) have forced comic strips to evolve differently than have their comic book cousins. The comic-strip-as-literature argument is not central to my paper, but I will note that comic strips are even lower on the literary totem pole than are comic books or graphic novels. A print resource on this topic might be nice, but I have not yet found a suitable one.

Liu, Jonathan H. "Comics as Literature, Part 1: The Usual Suspects." *WIRED*, June 1, 2012, https://is.gd/AOAaTA

This online article, by Jonathan Liu, lists a selection of comic books and graphic novels he considers to be literary. Liu is more fan than scholar, but his writing is well informed. He discusses *Watchmen* (written by Alan Moore), *Sandman* (written by Neil Gaiman), *Maus* (written by Art

Spiegelman), and *Understanding Comics* (written by Scott McCloud). Aside from providing useful summaries of the above comics, Liu's judgment about the literary merit of these works stands as an excellent example of populist insight into what "Joe Shmoe" considers to be literature.

McCloud, Scott. *Understanding Comics: The Invisible Art*. Harper Perennial, 1994.

This graphic novel, by Scott McCloud, is a foundational work in comic book and graphic novel studies. *Understanding Comics* makes a book-length argument about what comics are and how they evolved. Most of the research I read about graphic novels mentions this book, and for the definitional points in my paper ("What is a comic book?", "What is a graphic novel?"), I plan to adopt McCloud's thinking.

Understanding Comics has become an ingrained part of the conversation about comics and graphic novels, so I knew I had to read it. The chapters I plan to cite most heavily are "The Vocabulary of Comics" (great for definitional points); "Time Frames" (explaining how the passage of time is conveyed with panels); and "Show and Tell" (discussing how pictures and words came to intermingle, and why that intermingling is thought of as less intellectually demanding than words alone).

Miller, John Jackson, and Kate Willaert. *The ICv2-Comichron Comic Sales Report 2018*. 2019, https://is.gd/1JdS8u

This infographic, produced using data from *ICv2* (a geek culture website) and *Comichron* (a comics research website), provides comic sales information from 2014 to 2018 for the North American market. It divides its information into four distribution channels: comic stores, bookstores, digital markets, and other sales channels. This chart will help me establish that comics are increasingly being purchased through bookstores and that comic sales are trending upward year by year.

Miodrag, Hannah. "Comics and Literature." *The Routledge Companion to Comics*, edited by Frank Bramlett et al., Routledge, 2017, pp. 390–398.

In this book chapter, Hannah Miodrag discusses the prevailing popular, critical, and academic positions on comics-as-literature. Miodrag suggests that the most prominent comics scholars have often used literary or critical theory to ground their work. Though Miodrag's writing is colorless, her research is extensive. The sections "How Comics Critics Have Defined Literature" and "Comics and Literary Theory" will be helpful in analyzing the ways that comics scholarship has embraced literary theory.

OrionStarlancer. "Are Comics Literature?" *Comic Vine*, August 29, 2010, https://is.gd/0rpn5O

> This resource is a fan discussion on *Comic Vine* (a comics review website). As the title implies, the discussion pertains to whether comics should be considered literature. There are 40 distinct comments in the thread, with most comments voicing the opinion that comics should be considered literature. Some of the commentators provide evidence to support their position. Though I will not use this resource to bolster the central arguments in my paper, I will extract a few of the comments from this discussion to illustrate what some comic fans think about the comics-as-literature debate. I think comic book fans deserve a voice alongside comic book scholars, which is why I have decided to use this source.

Petersen, Robert S. "The Return of Graphic Narratives for Adults." *Comics, Manga, and Graphic Novels: A History of Graphic Narratives*, Praeger, 2011, pp. 205–226, https://is.gd/JegDAw

> This book chapter, by Robert Petersen, surveys the adult-and-alternative comics movements of the 1960s–1990s. In making the case that comics are literature, I plan to devote a section of my paper to the American alternative comics movement of the 1960s and the contemporaneous *bandes dessinées* style, popularized in France. This chapter discusses some of the key publications of these respective movements. Though many of the alternative and *bandes dessinées* publications were "adult" in the sense that they dabbled in erotica, many also spoke to controversial political and social themes. Their themes marked them as more "literary" than the mainstream comics of the day (which were written for unsophisticated juvenile audiences).

Spiegelman, Art. *Maus: A Survivor's Tale Part 1: My Father Bleeds History*. Penguin Books, 1987, https://is.gd/NVJAm7

> *Maus* is one of the works I plan to discuss to advance my argument that graphic novels should be considered literature. *Maus* tells the story of writer/artist Art Spiegelman's Jewish father, Vladek, who spent much of World War II (WWII) hiding from Nazi forces or imprisoned in concentration camps. Spiegelman draws *Maus* in a minimalist, black-and-white style and his characters are portrayed alternatively as human (in the current day) and animal (during WWII). To date, *Maus* is the only graphic novel to win a Pulitzer Prize (in the Special Award in Letters), which it was awarded in 1992. Though it did not win the Pulitzer Prize

for Fiction, I want to establish that *Maus'* story, technique, and artistry make it worthy of consideration as literature. To do this, I will also draw on Andrew Dale's analysis of *Maus* (*see* his entry in this annotated bibliography).

Spry, Adam. "Louis Riel: A Comic-Strip Biography." *Critical Survey of Graphic Novels: Independents and Underground Classics.*, edited by Bart Beaty and Stephen Weiner, 2nd ed., vol. 2, Salem Press, 2019, pp. 487–490.

This encyclopedia entry, by Adam Spry, summarizes and critiques the graphic novel *Louis Riel*, first published in 2003. Spry's entry contains the following sections: "Publication History," "Plot," "Characters," "Artistic Style," "Themes," and "Impact." Capturing the essence of an entire graphic novel is difficult, and so I will rely heavily on Spry's treatment.

There are two elements in *Louis Riel* that I will highlight when arguing for its status as literature. First, the author, Chester Brown, was responsible for every step of the graphic novel (writing, art, inking, lettering, drawing panel borders, etc.), which makes him very much like the sole author of a novel. Second, every page of *Louis Riel* features a layout of two columns and three rows, and this constancy mirrors the predictable page-by-page arrangement of literary prose. Spry provides the evidence I need to make these claims, so this is a great source to use as my second example of graphic-novel-as-literature.

Vie, Stephanie, and Brandy Dieterle. "Minding the Gap: Comics as Scaffolding for Critical Literacy Skills in the Classroom." *Composition Forum*, vol. 33, 2016, https://is.gd/atJwAw

This journal article discusses the use of two comic books – *Fun Home* by Alison Bechdel and *Y: The Last Man* by Brian Vaughn and Pia Guerrera – to promote critical literacy in a first-year writing course. Unfortunately, the authors do not discuss why these two comic books might be considered literature. Instead, they mostly engage in a discussion about how the comics could be used to develop critical literacy skills. I suppose applying critical literacy theory to these comics implies that the authors consider them literature, but the authors do not discuss the literary merits of the comics. I am not sure if I will use anything from this article in my paper, although it provides further evidence that comics are making their way into classrooms.

Wikimedia Foundation. "Classics Illustrated." *Wikipedia*, September 16, 2019. *Wikipedia*, https://is.gd/P9S6aH

> One argument I plan to make in my paper is that the *Classics Illustrated* line of comics – continually published since the 1940s – directly adapts literary works, and thus, the comics are themselves literature. I have heard my professors and librarians advise me not to cite *Wikipedia*, but this is the only complete listing I could find of all the *Classics Illustrated* titles. The information on this page will help me establish a history that shows comics' long association with literary material. Given that the information on this page is uncontroversial and a matter of public record, and given that I have used the "Permanent link" URL link in my citation, I feel safe in citing this page.

9.3 Sample Chicago Annotated Bibliography

I am writing a research paper about capital punishment in America. I do not have a working thesis yet, but I have found many sources about the death penalty in America, and my sense is that the death penalty is not being administered fairly. As this issue is hotly debated, I will ensure to present both sides of the debate.

Abili, Emily Jean. 2013. "A Historical Comparative Analysis of Executions in the United States from 1608 to 2009." Doctoral Dissertation, Las Vegas, NV: University of Nevada, Las Vegas (UNLV). https://is.gd/LdftTQ

> As per Abili, this doctoral dissertation "examines the history of executions, including lynchings, in the United States from 1608–2009" (2). In order to flesh out the historical background of my paper, I plan to use the chapters "Early America (1608–1815)" and "The Long 19th Century (1789–1920)." Though other works address capital punishment in early America, Abili's thesis is unique because it chronicles legal and extra-judicial killings, the latter of which are under-discussed in capital punishment scholarship. The other chapters do not interest me.

American Civil Liberties Union (ACLU). 2019. "Capital Punishment." ACLU. https://is.gd/ollJKq

> This webpage, written and compiled by the ACLU, provides readers with background information, news, and issue summaries related to the death penalty in America. As one would expect from the ACLU, a very liberal organization, the information is provocatively presented. The information is well referenced, however, so I believe it to be factual.

When I looked at the "Current Issues" section of the webpage, I found three articles that could be used in my paper: one article tells about the use of capital punishment on those with mental disabilities; another article discusses racial disparities in the application of capital sentencing; and a third article decries instances of prosecutorial misconduct. "The Latest" section of the webpage features a news feed highlighting new and popular stories about the death penalty.

Aratani, Lauren. 2018. "Capital Punishment in the US Continues Decline despite Slight Rise in 2018." *The Guardian*, December 14, 2018, sec. World news. https://is.gd/7Lsz70

This newspaper article, by Lauren Aratani, reports on the long-term decline of execution rates and capital convictions in the United States. Aratani notes that, since 1995, when public fears about criminality were at a peak, executions and capital trials lowered in number. Aratani also notes that the decline would have been sharper without the influence of Texas and Florida, who account for more than half of current US executions. The article also cites some opinion research which shows the US public is evenly split (± 5%) on whether there should be a death penalty and whether it is currently applied fairly and impartially. I will use some facts and figures from this article in my paper, and since *The Guardian* is an established and reputable newspaper, I have faith in the information.

Averill, Peg. 1976. *Capital Punishment Means Them Without the Capital Get the Punishment*. (Online image). https://is.gd/ag2LFb

This poster, illustrated by Peg Averill, was first produced in 1976. It features two prisoners – one swinging by his neck at the end of a rope, the other strapped into an electric chair – and the caption reads "capital punishment means them without the capital get the punishment." It effectively captures the inequities of capital sentencing, and I would like to include it as an image in my paper to forcefully illustrate that point.

Aviv, Rachel. 2015. "Revenge Killing: Race and the Death Penalty in a Louisiana Parish." *The New Yorker*, July 6, 2015. https://is.gd/xRV64P

In this magazine article, Rachel Aviv tells the story of Rodricus Crawford, a young man from Caddo Parish, Louisiana. Crawford was convicted – falsely, it would seem – of murdering his infant son. Caddo Parish is the most prolific county in the US for issuing death sentences, and Aviv blames systemic racism, biased policing, and an unstable prosecutor as the reasons for this. The reporting is powerful, and Aviv excellently balances national observations about capital punishment with the particulars of Crawford's case. I have chosen to use this article in my paper because it provides me with a contemporary case to discuss, and because it offers insights on the capriciousness of the death penalty.

Berns, Walter. 1979. "The Morality of Capital Punishment." In *For Capital Punishment: Crime and the Morality of the Death Penalty*, 153–176. New York: Basic Books. https://is.gd/djlMoE

In this book chapter, Walter Berns gives a wide-ranging account of why capital punishment should be thought of as a moral act. Though much of the chapter is given over to a feckless discussion of notable historical figures, the meat of the chapter contends that it is good and natural for a community to feel anger toward criminal perpetrators. Relatedly, Berns argues, it is also good and natural for this anger to be ratified via the exercise of capital punishments. I find this line of reasoning convincing, and while my paper argues against many aspects of capital sentencing, I will use some of Berns' points to acknowledge that capital punishment can be a justifiable punishment for major crimes. This chapter was very persuasive.

Brunello, Anthony R. 2016. "Politics, Ethics and Capital Punishment in America." *Review of History and Political Science* 4 (1): 13–30. https://is.gd/0h2B1l

This article, by Anthony Brunello, examines capital punishment in America. Brunello demonstrates that the death penalty, as currently practiced, is (1) neither swift nor sure; (2) neither fair nor equitable; (3) not cost-effective; and (4) not in line with global practices. He also chronicles the 1972–1976 moratorium on the death penalty. Though many sources discuss this period, Brunello's treatment is lucid and readable. The cases discussed are interesting, and so I might consult some newspapers from the moratorium period to learn more, but I will use Brunello in any case.

Congressional Research Service. 2016. *Federal Capital Offenses: An Abridged Overview of Substantive and Procedural Law*. Congressional Research Service. https://is.gd/kk9dNL

This report, authored by the Congressional Research Service, provides constitutional and legal information pertaining to capital punishment in America. The report has three sections: "Introduction," "Constitutional

Considerations," and "Existing Federal Law." The last section includes a comprehensive discussion of death-eligible offenses. As the Congressional Research Service is trustworthy, and the report is quite recent, I plan to use much of this information to contextualize my paper. I have not found this information so succinctly in another source.

Death Penalty Information Center. 2019. "News & Developments." Death Penalty Information Center. https://is.gd/9obJmQ

On its "About Us" page, The Death Penalty Information Center (DPIC) describes itself as "a national non-profit organization serving the media and the public with analysis and information on issues concerning capital punishment." Though in name the DPIC eschews an advocacy position, in spirit it is committed to publishing information critical of the death penalty, so it is biased. However, the DPIC has thoroughly supported its claims with data, and it refers to outside sources, so I can be confident in its information. The "News & Developments" section doubles as the DPIC's homepage, and the contents of this section change daily. I imagine I will use multiple resources from the DPIC website, but I have not decided which ones.

Isonhood, Lindy Lou. 2018. *A Juror's Reflections on the Death Penalty*. Video file. TED Conferences, LLC. https://is.gd/YpKHzZ

In this TED Talk, Lindy Lou Isonhood recounts her experience as a capital trial juror. She and her fellow jurors sentenced a man to die, and in the intervening years, Isonhood dealt with the psychological weight of her vote. After years of deep personal reflection, Isonhood now opposes capital punishment and publicly advocates against it. In my research, I have found no other sources that examine the burden placed on capital trial juries. Though I do not anticipate giving much room in my paper to the experience of juries, I can use Isonhood's story because it humanizes the juror's role in capital sentencing. I anticipate using it in my section on ethics/morality of the death penalty.

Lyon, Andrea D. 2015. "The Death Penalty Yesterday and Today." In *The Death Penalty: What's Keeping It Alive?*, 1–21. Rowman & Littlefield.

Andrea Lyon's book chapter relates a history of the death penalty in America from 1607 to 2015. The chapter highlights landmark decisions, philosophical considerations, and procedural issues related to death penalty sentencing. As a history, this chapter provides a readable overview of the death penalty in America; as a critique of the death penalty, the chapter highlights post-conviction acquittals, differing standards of evidence, cost-effectiveness of the death penalty, and other issues. Lyon's analysis will help me build the background section of my paper.

Mandery, Evan J. 2013. *A Wild Justice: The Death and Resurrection of Capital Punishment in America*. New York: W. W. Norton & Company.

> This book, by Evan Mandery, explores the 1972 Supreme Court decision *Furman* v. *Georgia*, in which the Court ruled that capital punishment violated the Eighth Amendment's prohibition against cruel and unusual punishment. Though detailed in its portrayal of the justices, caselaw, and political climate of the time, the book is also written in a fast-paced and engaging style. Perhaps Mandery's background as a fiction writer contributes to this style. This book provides a wonderful account of *Furman* v. *Georgia* and the ensuing four-year moratorium on capital punishment. To close the book, Mandery covers the 1976 case *Gregg* v. *Georgia*, which ushered in the return of the death penalty. This is the most thorough resource I have found on why the death penalty was struck down, and subsequently overturned, in the 1970s.

Masci, David. 2018. "5 Facts about the Death Penalty." *Pew Research Center* (blog). August 2, 2018. https://is.gd/h29ndq

> This summary of a Pew Research Center study, by David Masci, highlights five facts about American opinion of the death penalty. The Pew Research Center is renowned for its high-quality research, and I plan to use data from fact #4 ("There are racial, gender, religious and political divides in opinions on the death penalty in the U.S."). I believe this data will flesh out my arguments about popular sentiment and the death penalty. I also plan to use one piece of information from fact #5 ("Americans harbor doubts about how the death penalty is applied and whether it deters serious crime"). Fact #5 shows that 71% of Americans believe there is a significant risk that innocent people will be sentenced to death. I think this will help demonstrate that many Americans mistrust capital punishment.

Palmer, Louis J. 2008. "Death-Eligible Offenses." In *Encyclopedia of Capital Punishment in the United States*, 2nd ed., 141–142. Jefferson, N.C: McFarland & Company.

> This encyclopedia article lists and defines death-eligible offenses in the United States. Death-eligible offenses are "crimes that are punishable with death … [as] not every murder justifies the consideration of capital punishment" (p. 141). In my paper I plan to create a bulleted list of death-eligible offenses in the United States. Here is a partial list containing examples of murder types I might consider in my paper:

- Premeditated murder
- Felony murder (murder while committing another crime)
- Victim-specific murder (targeting workers in occupations that are presumed to be hostile to criminals, e.g., police, prison guards, etc.)
- Murder-for-hire
- Selling illegal drugs that result in death
- Drive-by-shootings that result in death
- Specific-device murder (using an illegal device to murder someone)
- Hostage murder
- Multiple-victim murder
- Drug-trafficking murder
- Murder on the run (committed while escaping from law enforcement or lawful custody)

Steiker, Carol S., and Jordan M. Steiker. 2016. "The Future of the American Death Penalty." In *Courting Death: The Supreme Court and Capital Punishment*, 255–289. Cambridge, Massachusetts: The Belknap Press of Harvard University Press.

This book chapter, by Carol Steiker and Jordan Steiker, discusses the legal future of capital punishment in America. The authors contend that, because of constitutional factors, the probability is low for a federally imposed abolition of the death penalty. They also note that, politically speaking, it would be unpalatable for states like Texas or Alabama to abolish capital punishment any time soon. The authors suggest, however, that the Eighth Amendment's proportionality test might be a constitutional avenue to pursue abolition. (I plan to look up the Eighth Amendment to understand what the authors mean.)

Though I am not a legal scholar, the authors' arguments seem sound, and they present straightforward and credible evidence for their claims. As I will devote a section of my paper to the future of the death penalty, I will certainly cite some of this chapter. I will also talk about the Marshall Hypothesis, which the authors explain is the contention that the American public would oppose the death penalty if they were fully informed about it. This is the first source I have found discussing the Marshall Hypothesis, and I would like to mention it in my introduction or conclusion.

Stogner, Maggie Burnette. 2018. *In the Executioner's Shadow: A Film about Justice, Injustice and the Death Penalty.* Video file. New Day Films. https://is.gd/zpnVsj

> This 2018 documentary highlights the stories of a former executioner, a victim in the Boston Marathon bombing, and the parents of a murdered woman who oppose the death penalty. Each of the respective parties has misgivings about the administration of the death penalty in the United States, and the filmmakers contextualize these concerns with additional facts and commentary.
>
> While the documentary is critical of the status of capital sentencing, the film is nonetheless even-handed. The protagonists go into depth when telling their stories, and no easy solutions are given. I found the story of the former executioner particularly moving, and I would like to refer to his experiences. I think the Isonhood TED Talk (see above) would pair well with this source.

The Constitution Project. 2014. *Irreversible Error: Recommended Reforms for Preventing and Correcting Errors in the Administration of Capital Punishment.* Washington, DC: The Constitution Project. https://is.gd/FcCl7P

> This book, by The Constitution Project, contains 12 chapters and two appendices on "improving the accuracy and fairness of capital trials" (p. xvii). The Constitution Project is a non-profit organization that "promotes constitutional rights and values by forging a non-ideological consensus aimed at sound legal interpretations and policy solutions" (p. iii). The chapters I plan to use in my research are "Safeguarding Innocence and Preventing Wrongful Execution"; "Safeguarding Racial Fairness and Proportionality"; "Role of Prosecutors"; and "Appendix II: Death Penalty Statistics."
>
> *Irreversible Error* makes 39 recommendations to promote increased fairness and safeguards for capital trials. The book's recommendations are i nformed by contextual information, evidence, and relevant case law in the United States. I feel safe in incorporating some of the book's recommendations into my paper because The Constitution Project is a nonpartisan organization. I will use the chapters identified earlier to highlight key issues in the debate over US capital punishment.

Von Drehle, David. 2015. "Execution in America." *Time*, June 8, 2015. https://is.gd/Nf3rWG

> In this magazine article, David Von Drehle outlines five reasons why the use of capital punishment in America is on the decline. Von Drehle's reasons are: (1) that legally killing is institutionally and mechanically difficult; (2) that America's crime rate is declining and is expected to further decline in the foreseeable future; (3) that executions are cost-ineffective; (4) that capital punishment was historically used to enforce a system of white supremacy; and (5) that most judges and prosecutors acknowledge that the application of the death penalty is essentially random. Given Von Drehle's history with capital punishment – he wrote the 1996 book, *Among the Lowest of the Dead: Inside Death Row* – this author has high credibility and I trust his conclusions.

Zivot, Joel B. 2012. "The Absence of Cruelty Is Not the Presence of Humanness: Physicians and the Death Penalty in the United States." *Philosophy, Ethics, and Humanities in Medicine* 7 (1): 7:13 1–4. https://is.gd/8K68Ou

> This medical commentary, by Joel Zivot, argues that physicians have no ethical obligation to participate in legal executions. Unfortunately, many lethal injections – now the standard method of execution – are botched and cause undue suffering. Though some physicians wish to reduce this unnecessary suffering by overseeing executions, Zivot argues that physician involvement in executions is unethical because it does not promote life and runs contrary to accepted medical practice. He also notes that the American Medical Association's code of ethics expressly forbids physician participation in executions. Zivot's reasoning and conclusions are sound, and I trust the factuality of his claims.

GLOSSARY

abstract   a written summary, typically one or two paragraphs, of a scholarly article, book, or speech, that provides a concise overview of the scholarly work's context or purpose, main points and key arguments, problem or major research question(s), thesis/hypothesis, methods, findings, and conclusions. (See **precis**, **synopsis**)

American Psychological Association (APA)   a professional organization of researchers, clinicians, educators, and students in psychology.

annotate   the act of taking notes on or about a text or other artifact.

annotated bibliography   an organized list of citations wherein each citation is annotated; typically alphabetized, though it can be arranged in other logical ways.

annotation   a note about a source; the five annotation types are descriptive, summative, evaluative, reflective, and combined.

bibliographic essay   a special form of a literature review that summarizes relevant research in an organized list within a continuous prose narrative.

bibliographic information   information that identifies source texts and that varies with the citation style being used, including information such as author, publisher, page numbers, publisher, date of publication, date of access.

bibliography   an organized list of citations, most often presented alphabetically, including entries that identify all the information needed to locate the listed sources. In in APA-style papers, called **References**; MLA-style papers, called **Works Cited**; in Chicago-style papers, called **Bibliography**.

Bibliography   the name for a list of references in the Chicago style (and some other documentation styles).

book review   a work that describes, summarizes, and critiques a book.

Chicago a style of documenting sources and a guide for formatting and editing formal written work, including academic writing. (See **Turabian**)

citation a written identifier of a source used in a text, whether in a footnote, endnote, in-text citation, or bibliography. (See **reference**)

citation style a format for documenting sources used in a text and in a bibliography of any kind. (See **documentation style**)

cite to identify the origin of a source in a footnote, endnote, in-text citation, or bibliography.

combined annotation one of the five annotation types; uses at least two, and up to all four, of the other annotation types (descriptive, summative, evaluative, and reflective).

comprehensive literature review a narrative of relevant scholarship on a given topic that summarizes, evaluates, and synthesizes all important works to date on that topic, critically appraising the scholarship under review (See **literature review, systematic literature review**)

descriptive annotation one of the five annotation types (the others are summative, evaluative, reflective, and combined); a note that informs readers about the basic nature of a resource, typically listing features of the work, including the creators, content, composition, publication format, and other pertinent details.

Digital Object Identifier (DOI) a unique code made of numbers, letters, and symbols used to permanently identify a document and link to it on the Internet; helps readers easily locate a cited document.

documentation style The set of guidelines for citing sources; the formatting guidelines for bibliographies and other scholarly writing; many are associated with particular fields of study and professions. (See **citation style**)

endnote a citation that appears at the end of a paper, chapter, or book. (See **footnote, in-text citation**)

evaluative annotation one of the five annotation types (the others are descriptive, summative, reflective, and combined); judges the trustworthiness, reliability, and value of a source and its creator(s).

footnote a citation that appears at the bottom of a page of text and/or images. (See **endnote, in-text citation**)

hanging paragraph format a typed passage whose first line is flush left (not indented) but whose other lines are indented, typically by a half-inch.

indirect quotation a reference to a secondary source that a writer did not read but that the writer wants to use after having found the work quoted by a primary source. (See **quotation**)

in-text citation a reference to a source in the body of a text. (See **endnote, footnote**)

literature review a narrative summary of the scholarship on a given topic; most include only the most important and relevant scholarship, critically appraising the scholarship under review. (See **comprehensive literature review**, **systematic literature review**)

Modern Language Association (MLA)   an organization of humanities scholars, including professionals and students in Comparative Literature, English Studies, Foreign Languages and Literatures, Literary Criticism and Cultural Studies.

organizational mode   the logical principle by which a text is ordered, such as comparison–contrast, cause–effect, and classification.

organizational principle   a rule or guideline by which one arranges information in a text.

paraphrase   to reword a passage from a source.

permalink   a permanent and unchanging link to an online source.

plagiarism   the use of someone's work (words or ideas) without acknowledging the source.

precis   a summary or abstract of a text or speech that offers a concise digest of the work. Commonly used in the business world and some academic disciplines. (See **abstract**, **synopsis**)

prefatory matter   an introduction to the topic and scope of a work; appears at the beginning of an annotated bibliography, book, proposal, or research paper; may include a thesis statement.

preliminary annotated bibliography   a simplified version of an annotated bibliography, often including brief descriptive annotations and sometimes also including reflective and/or evaluative annotations.

quotation   a passage taken word for word from another source.

reference   another word for citation; a written identifier of a source, whether in a footnote, endnote, in-text citation, or bibliography. (See **citation)**

References   the name of a bibliography in APA-style scholarship (and in some other documentation styles).

reflective annotation   one of the five annotation types (the others are descriptive, summative, evaluative, and combined); tells where and how one might use a source in research writing or other professional work.

research paper   an essay in which a writer uses sources, citations, and a bibliography to support a thesis.

rhetorical purpose   the intention of an author for a text regarding the effect on readers; typically, texts have one of four types (inform, explain, argue/persuade, or entertain) or are multi-purposed.

source   any outside material used in research and other forms of writing.

source feature   the layout and other elements of a source, including the way it uses headings, pagination, and so on.

summative annotation   one of the five annotation types (the others are descriptive, evaluative, reflective, and combined; a note about a source that recaps the main points or arguments of the source.

synopsis   an abstract or summary of a work, often applied to artistic works.

systematic literature review a literature review that summarizes, evaluates, and synthesizes scholarship in a methodical manner, critically appraising the scholarship under review. (See **comprehensive literature review**, **literature review**)

Turabian a citation method devised by Kate Turabian to simplify the Chicago style for students writing research papers.

webpage a single page/document on a website.

website a collection of webpages on the Internet.

Works Cited the name of a bibliography in Chicago and MLA papers (and in some other documentation styles).

workspace a convenient location for keeping notes organized.

UNIFIED LIST OF WORKS CITED, EXAMPLES, AND FURTHER READINGS

Aaron, Jane E., and Ellen Kuhl Repetto. *The Compact Reader: Short Essays by Method and Theme*, 11th ed., St. Martins, Bedford, 2019.

Abili, Emily Jean. *A Historical Comparative Analysis of Executions in the United States from 1608 to 2009*, University of Nevada, Las Vegas (UNLV), 2013, https://is.gd/LdftTQ

Aesop, et al. *The Fables of Aesop Paraphras'd in Verse: Adorn'd with Sculpture, and Illustrated with Annotations*, Thomas Roycroft, 1668, https://is.gd/gO83lp

Allocca, Kevin. *Videocracy: How YouTube Is Changing the World … With Double Rainbows, Singing Foxes, and Other Trends We Can't Stop Watching*, Bloomsbury, 2018.

American Civil Liberties Union (ACLU). "Capital Punishment." *American Civil Liberties Union (ACLU)*, 2019, https://is.gd/ollJKq

American Medical Association, editor. *AMA Manual of Style: A Guide for Authors and Editors*, 11th ed., Oxford University Press, 2020.

American Psychological Association, editor. *Publication Manual of the American Psychological Association*, 6th ed., American Psychological Association, 2010.

American Psychological Association. "APA Style Blog." APA Style Blog, 2019, https://is.gd/CVuhnf

American Sociological Association, editor. *American Sociological Association Style Guide*, 6th ed., American Sociological Association, 2019.

Anker, Susan. *Real Writing with Readings: Paragraphs and Essays for Success in College, Work, and Everyday Life*, 8th ed., St. Martins, Bedford, 2019.

Aratani, Lauren. "Capital Punishment in the US Continues Decline despite Slight Rise in 2018." *The Guardian*, 14 Dec. 2018, https://is.gd/7Lsz70

Arora, Sanjeev, and Institute for Advanced Study. "Brief Introduction to Deep Learning and the 'Alchemy' Controversy." 2019, https://is.gd/yajq2t

Ashcraft, Mark H. "Models of Math Anxiety." *Mathematics Anxiety: What Is Known and What Is Still to Be Understood*, edited by Irene C. Mammarella et al., Routledge, 2019, pp. 1–19.

Association for Psychological Science. "Math Anxiety Doesn't Equal Poor Math Performance." *APS – Association for Psychological Science*, 4 Nov. 2015, https://is.gd/AXzyzO

Averill, Peg. *Capital Punishment Means Them without the Capital Get the Punishment.* 1976, https://is.gd/ag2LFb

Aviv, Rachel. "Revenge Killing: Race and the Death Penalty in a Louisiana Parish." *The New Yorker*, vol. 91, no. 19, July. 2015, pp. 32–38, https://is.gd/xRV64P

Babcock, Rebecca Day, and Sharifa Daniels. *Writing Centers and Disability*, Fountainhead Press, 2017.

Balsamo, Luigi. *Bibliography: History of a Tradition*, B.M. Rosenthal, 1990.

Bankole, Katherine Olukemi. "Creation." *Encyclopedia of African Religion*, edited by Molefi Kete Asante, and Ama Mazama, SAGE 2009, pp. 184–186, https://is.gd/NBAfiQ

Beilock, Sian L., and Daniel T. Willingham. "Math Anxiety: Can Teachers Help Students Reduce It?" *American Educator*, vol. 38, no. 2, 2014, pp. 28–32, https://is.gd/1nZQwH

Bell, Emily. "Research Guides: Citation and Research Management Tools at Harvard: Comparing Citation Tools." *Harvard University*, 4 Dec. 2019, https://is.gd/ZhLSbn

Berns, Walter. "The Morality of Capital Punishment." *For Capital Punishment: Crime and the Morality of the Death Penalty*, Basic Books, 1979, pp. 153–176, https://is.gd/djlMoE

Blijden, Judith. *The Accuracy of Rights Statements on Europeana.Eu.* Kennisland, 2018, https://is.gd/BYn5Ak

Booth, Andrew, et al. *Systematic Approaches to a Successful Literature Review*, 2nd ed., SAGE, 2016.

Brunello, Anthony R. "Politics, Ethics and Capital Punishment in America." *Review of History and Political Science*, vol. 4, no. 1, 2016, pp. 13–30, https://is.gd/0h2B1l

Bui, Yvonne N. *How to Write a Master's Thesis*, 2nd ed., SAGE, 2014.

Burkle-Young, Francis A., and Saundra Maley. *The Art of the Footnote[1]: The Intelligent Student's Guide to the Art and Science of Annotating Texts*, University Press of America, 1996.

Calabrese, Raymond L. *The Dissertation Desk Reference: The Doctoral Student's Manual to Writing the Dissertation*, Rowman & Littlefield Education, 2009.

Calvani, Mayra, and Anne K. Edwards. *The Slippery Art of Book Reviewing*, Twilight Times Books, 2008.

Campbell, W. Joseph. "The Rise and Fall of Netscape." *Baltimore Sun*, 8 Aug. 2016, https://is.gd/eqKWfx

Canada, Statistics. "History of the Canadian Labour Force Survey, 1945–2016: Chart 2 – Participation Rate by Sex, 1946-2015." *Statistics Canada*, Jan. 2017, https://is.gd/FVfvVB

Cave, Roderick, and Sara Ayad. *The History of the Book in 100 Books: The Complete Story, from Egypt to e-Book*, Firefly Books, Inc., 2014.

Chernin, Eli. "The 'Harvard System': A Mystery Dispelled." *British Medical Journal*, vol. 297, no. 6655, Oct. 1988, pp. 1062–1063, https://is.gd/3wi4Hc

Chinn, Stephen J. *The Trouble with Maths: A Practical Guide to Helping Learners with Numeracy Difficulties*, 2nd ed., Routledge, 2012.

Choe, Jaeyeon, and McNally John. "Buddhism in the United States: An Ethnographic Study." *International Journal of Religious Tourism and Pilgrimage*, vol. 1, no. 1, 2013, https://is.gd/DYKzEH

Chute, Hillary L. "Comics for Grown-Ups?" *Why Comics? from Underground to Everywhere*, Harper, 2017, pp. 1–32.

Cleaver, Samantha. "Comics & Graphic Novels." *Instructor*, vol. 117, no. 6, 2008, pp. 28–34, https://is.gd/Y2zeOM

Cochran, Jessica. "Let's Do It! the Center for Book and Paper Arts: A History." *The Journal of Artists' Books*, vol. 46, no. Fall, 2019, pp. 3–13.

Cochran, Philip. "Big Fish Stories: Analysis of Historical Newspaper Data on Size of Lake Sturgeon (Acipenser Fulvescens) in the Lake Michigan Basin." *Michigan Academician*, vol. 42, no. 1, 2015, pp. 26–39.

Cochran, Randy. *Critter Golf: The Adventures at Owl's Nest*, Outskirts Press, 2013.

Coghill, Anne M., and Lorrin R. Garson, editors. *The ACS Style Guide: Effective Communication of Scientific Information*, 3rd ed., Oxford University Press, 2006.

Cohen, Norm. "The Folk and Popular Roots of Country Music." *The Encyclopedia of Country Music*, edited by Paul Kingsbury et al., 2nd ed., Oxford University Press, 2012, pp. 176–180, https://is.gd/nsOqzL

Colaianne, Anthony Joseph. "The Aims and Methods of Annotated Bibliography." *Scholarly Publishing*, vol. 11, no. 4, 1980, pp. 321–331.

Coles, Terri. "How Teens Can Fight Math Anxiety." *Bright Magazine*, Apr. 2017, https://is.gd/LxsP4f

Columbia, Law Review, et al., editors. *The Bluebook: A Uniform System of Citation*, 20th ed., The Harvard Law Review Association, 2015.

Congressional Research Service. "English as the Official Language of the United States: Legal Background." *Congressional Research Service*, 23 Dec. 2010, pp. 1–10, https://is.gd/nvrEw4

Congressional Research Service. "Federal Capital Offenses: An Abridged Overview of Substantive and Procedural Law." *Congressional Research Service*, 2016, https://is.gd/kk9dNL

Connors, Robert J. "The Rhetoric of Citation Systems, Part I: The Development of Annotation Structures from the Renaissance to 1900." *Rhetoric Review*, vol. 17, no. 1, 1998, pp. 6–48.

Cope, Bill, and Angus Phillips, editors. *The Future of the Academic Journal*, 2nd ed., Chandos Publishing, 2014.

Council of Science Editors. *Scientific Style and Format: The CSE Manual for Authors, Editors, and Publishers*, 8th ed., University of Chicago Press, 2014.

Cox, Howard, and Simon Mowatt. *Revolutions from Grub Street: A History of Magazine Publishing in Britain*, 1st ed., Oxford University Press, 2014.

Dale, Andrew. *Graphic Novels: Essential Literary Genres*, Abdo Publishing, 2017.

Daniels, Barbara. *Street Children and Philanthropy in the Second Half of the Nineteenth Century*. The Open University, 2008, https://is.gd/M7i1cU

Davies, Eryl W. "The Bible in Ethics." *The Oxford Handbook of Biblical Studies*, edited by J. W. Rogerson, and Judith M. Lieu, Oxford University Press, 2006, pp. 732–753, https://is.gd/C0YD0o

Death Penalty Information Center. "News & Developments." *Death Penalty Information Center*, 2019, https://is.gd/9obJmQ

Dixon, Wheeler W., and Gwendolyn Audrey Foster. *A Short History of Film*, 3rd ed., Rutgers University Press, 2018.

Doedens-Plant, Anna, and Clara Rindeline. *An Investigation into the Associations between Maths Anxiety in Secondary School Pupils and Teachers' and Parents' Implicit Theories of Intelligence and Failure*, University of Southampton, 2018, https://is.gd/ihm1mp

Dombrowksi, Quinn. "Drupal and Other Content Management Systems." *Doing Digital Humanities: Practice, Training, Research*, edited by Constance Crompton et al., Routledge, 2016, pp. 289–302.

Doré, Gustave. "The Tower of Babel." *The Doré Bible Gallery*, 1892, https://is.gd/8FetwS

Dowd, Michelle M. "Household Pedagogies: Female Educators and the Language of Legacy." *Women's Work in Early Modern English Literature and Culture, Palgrave Macmillan*, 2009, pp. 133–172, https://is.gd/td5x1A

Dowker, Ann, and Peter Morris. "Targeted Interventions for Children with Difficulties in Learning Mathematics." *The Routledge International Handbook of Dyscalculia and Mathematical Learning Difficulties*, edited by Steve Chinn, 2017, pp. 256–264.

Dubner, Stephen J. "What Do Nancy Pelosi, Taylor Swift, and Serena Williams Have in Common?" (Ep. 385). *Freakonomics, LLC*, 17 July 2019, https://is.gd/Cc88od

Efron, Sara Efrat, and Ruth Ravid. *Writing the Literature Review: A Practical Guide*, The Guilford Press, 2019.

El Khatib, Randa, et al. "Open Social Scholarship Annotated Bibliography." *KULA: Knowledge Creation, Dissemination, and Preservation Studies*, vol. 3, no. 1, 2019, article 24, pp. 1–141, https://is.gd/CXcocY

Eliot, Simon, and Jonathan Rose, editors. *A Companion to the History of the Book*, Blackwell Pub, 2007.

Emina, Seb. "In France, Comic Books Are Serious Business." *The New York Times*, 29 Jan. 2019, https://is.gd/KKGEUd

Enos, Richard Leo. *Greek Rhetoric before Aristotle*, 2nd ed., Parlor Press, 2011.

Eula, Michael J., and Janet Madden. *Compiling the Annotated Bibliography: A Guide*, 2nd ed., Kendall/Hunt Pub. C., 1995.

Feynman, Richard, et al. "The Feynman Lectures on Physics." *The Feynman Lectures on Physics*, California Institute of Technology, 2013, https://is.gd/lV8iuh

Fichtelberg, Aaron. *Hybrid Tribunals: A Comparative Examination*, Springer, 2015, https://is.gd/Id1gda

Fitzpatrick, Damian, and Tracey Costley. "Using Annotated Bibliographies to Develop Student Writing in Social Sciences." *Discipline-Specific Writing: Theory into Practice*, edited by John Flowerdew, and Tracey Costley, Routledge, 2017, pp. 113–125.

Flood, Alison. "JRR Tolkien Translation of Beowulf to Be Published after 90-Year Wait." *The Guardian*, 19 Mar. 2014, https://is.gd/WIzDVv

Gall, Elisa, and Patrick Gall. "Comics Are Picture Books: A (Graphic) Novel Idea." *Horn Book Magazine*, vol. 91, no. 6, Dec. 2015, pp. 45–50.

Gardner, Helen, and Fred S. Kleiner. *Gardner's Art through the Ages: A Global History*, 16th ed., Cengage Learning, 2020.

Gardner, Jared. *The Rise and Fall of Early American Magazine Culture*, University of Illinois Press, 2012.

Gatten, Jeffrey N. *Woodstock Scholarship: An Interdisciplinary Annotated Bibliography*, Open Book Publishers, 2016, https://is.gd/nZ5GwM

Gazzoni, Andrea. "Mapping Dante: A Digital Platform for the Study of Places in the Commedia." *Humanist Studies & the Digital Age*, vol. 5, no. 1, 2017, pp. 83–96, https://is.gd/1B6PLb

Gerstein Science Information Centre. "Research Guides: Citation Management: Comparison Table." *University of Toronto Libraries*, 23 Jan. 2019, https://is.gd/jzZAa6

Gibaldi, Joseph, editor. *MLA Style Manual and Guide to Scholarly Publishing*, 3rd ed., Modern Language Association of America, 2008.

Gooding, Paul. *Historic Newspapers in the Digital Age: "Search All about It!"*, Routledge, 2017.

Gupta, Arun. "The Tea Party of No." *The Indypendent*, vol. 157, Oct. 2010, pp. 8–9, 12, https://is.gd/y4FgLX

Hacker, Diana, and Nancy I. Sommers. *A Pocket Style Manual*, 8th ed., Bedford/St Martin's, 2018.

Hainsworth, Peter. "From Dante to Umberto Eco: Why Read Italian Literature?" *OUPblog*, 8 June 2012, https://is.gd/PryUgz

Hansen, Kathleen A., and Nora Paul. *Future-Proofing the News: Preserving the First Draft of History*, Rowman & Littlefield, 2017.

Harmon, Robert B. *Elements of Bibliography: A Guide to Information Sources and Practical Applications*, 3rd ed., Scarecrow Press, 1998.

Harner, James L. *On Compiling an Annotated Bibliography*, 2nd ed., Modern Language Association of America, 2000.

Harvard Divinity School. "Four Principles: Differentiating between Devotional Expression and the Study of Religion." *Religious Literacy Project*, 2019, https://is.gd/Lv0Cl7

Harvey, Gordon. *Writing with Sources: A Guide for Students*, 3rd ed., Hackett Publishing Company, Inc, 2017.

Hauptman, Robert. *Documentation: A History and Critique of Attribution, Commentary, Glosses, Marginalia, Notes, Bibliographies, Works-Cited Lists, and Citation Indexing and Analysis*, McFarland, 2008.

Hendricks, John Allen, and Bruce Mims. *The Radio Station: Broadcasting, Podcasting, and Streaming*, 10th ed., Routledge, 2018.

Hering, Heike. *How to Write Technical Reports: Understandable Structure, Good Design, Convincing Presentation*, Springer, 2019.

Hockney, David, and Martin Gayford. *A History of Pictures: From the Cave to the Computer Screen*, Abrams, 2016.

Houston, Keith. *The Book: A Cover-to-Cover Exploration of the Most Powerful Object of Our Time. W.W*, Norton & Company, 2016.

Husband, Tony, editor. *Cartoons of World War II*, Arcturus, 2013, https://is.gd/SWVlUk

Hutton, Robert. *Comics and Literature: A Love Story*, Carleton University, 2017, https://is.gd/dNw6CO

Hyland, Ken, and Giuliana Diani, editors. *Academic Evaluation: Review Genres in University Settings*, Palgrave Macmillan, 2009.

Internal Revenue Service. "IRS History Timeline." *Internal Revenue Service*, Mar. 2019, pp. 1–48, https://is.gd/mMDmFx

International Organization for Standardization. "ISO 214:1976(En), Documentation—Abstracts for Publications and Documentation." *ISO Online Browsing Platform (OBP)*, 1976/2019, https://is.gd/zoI2iK

Isonhood, Lindy Lou. *A Juror's Reflections on the Death Penalty*, TED Conferences, LLC, 2018, https://is.gd/YpKHzZ

Jennings, Kimberly Ann, et al. "Fifth Graders' Enjoyment, Interest, and Comprehension of Graphic Novels Compared to Heavily-Illustrated and Traditional Novels." *International Electronic Journal of Elementary Education*, vol. 6(2), 2014, pp. 257–274, https://is.gd/Z0cMqt

Jesson, Jill, et al. *Doing Your Literature Review: Traditional and Systematic Techniques*, SAGE, 2011.

Jones, Inigo, et al. *The Most Notable Antiquity of Great Britain, Vulgarly Called Stone-Heng, on Salisbury Plain*, James Flesher, 1655, https://is.gd/x8HJQ9

Justo, Luís Pereira, and Helena Maria Calil. "Relationships between Mood Disorders and Substance Abuse during Adolescence." *Drug Abuse in Adolescence: Neurobiological, Cognitive, and Psychological Issues*, edited by Denise De Micheli et al., Springer, 2016, pp. 173–195, https://is.gd/0bJokH

Kafker, Frank A., and Jeff Loveland, editors. *The Early Britannica (1768-1803): The Growth of an Outstanding Encyclopedia*, Voltaire Foundation, 2009.

Kasperiuniene, Judita, and Vilma Zydziunaite. "A Systematic Literature Review on Professional Identity Construction in Social Media." *SAGE Open*, vol. 9, no. 1, 2019, pp. 1–11, https://is.gd/lpKz9b

Kellett, Dave, and Frederick Schroeder. *Stripped*. Sequential Films, 2014, https://is.gd/HVmMom

Klass, Perri. "Fending off Math Anxiety." *The New York Times*, 24 Apr. 2017, p. 4, https://is.gd/gkiSfu

Kmiec, David, and Bernadette Longo. *The IEEE Guide to Writing in the Engineering and Technical Fields*, John Wiley and Sons, Inc, 2017.

Koenig, Gaspard. "Do We Really Own Our Bodies?" *TEDxParis*, 13 Sept. 2016, https://is.gd/KbcwBW

König, Jason, and Greg Woolf, editors. *Encyclopaedism from Antiquity to the Renaissance*, Cambridge University Press, 2013.

Kosseff, Jeff. *The Twenty-Six Words that Created the Internet*, Cornell University Press, 2019.

Kranzler, John H. *Statistics for the Terrified*, 6th ed., Rowman & Littlefield, 2018.

Krummel, Donald William. *Bibliographies, Their Aims and Methods*, H.W. Wilson Co., 1984.

Lagasse, Paul. "Airline Industry." *Encyclopedia of American Business History*, edited by Charles R. Geisst, Vol. 1, Facts on File, Inc., 2006, pp. 9–12, https://is.gd/DC8Eh8

Lasky, Jack, editor. *The Internet*, Greenhaven Press, 2016.

Lavik, Erlend. "Romantic Authorship in Copyright Law and the Uses of Aesthetics." *Work of Authorship*, edited by Mireille Van Eechoud, and Amsterdam University Press, 2015, pp. 45–93, https://is.gd/qIJpJJ

Leccese, Mark, and Jerry Lanson. *The Elements of Blogging: Expanding the Conversation of Journalism*, Focal Press, 2016.

Lee, Mordecai. *The First Presidential Communications Agency: FDR's Office of Government Reports*, State University of New York Press, 2005.

Leggatt, Alexander. "Playhouses, Stages and Performances." *Jacobean Public Theatre*, Routledge, 2005, pp. 9–25, https://is.gd/6EikXA

Lester, James D., and James D. Lester, Jr. *Writing Research Papers: A Complete Guide*, 15th ed., Pearson, 2018.

Library of Congress. "A Brief Introduction to the Music of Aaron Copland." *Library of Congress*, 2019, https://is.gd/gjIjD4

Linsenmayer, Mark. "Pretty Much Pop #2: Binge Watching." *The Partially Examined Life, LLC*, 23 July 2019, https://is.gd/GgYqnx

Lipson, Charles. *How to Write A BA Thesis: A Practical Guide from Your First Ideas to Your Finished Paper*, 2nd ed., The University of Chicago Press, 2018.

Liu, Jonathan H. "Comics as Literature, Part 1: The Usual Suspects." *WIRED*, 1 June 2012, https://is.gd/AOAaTA

Lynch, Jack. *You Could Look It Up: The Reference Shelf from Ancient Babylon to Wikipedia*, Bloomsbury Press, 2016.

Lyon, Andrea D. "The Death Penalty Yesterday and Today." *The Death Penalty: What's Keeping It Alive*, Rowman & Littlefield, 2015, pp. 1–21.

Mandery, Evan J. *A Wild Justice: The Death and Resurrection of Capital Punishment in America*, W. W. Norton & Company, 2013.

Masci, David. "5 Facts about the Death Penalty." *Pew Research Center*, 2 Aug. 2018, https://is.gd/h29ndq

Matthew, W. D. *Dinosaurs with Special Reference to the American Museum Collections. American Museum of Natural History*, 1915, https://is.gd/Ir8sMa

McCloud, Scott. *Understanding Comics: The Invisible Art*, Harper Perennial, 1994.

Miller, John Jackson, and Kate Willaert. *The ICv2-Comichron Comic Sales Report 2018*. 2019, https://is.gd/1JdS8u

Miodrag, Hannah. "Comics and Literature." *The Routledge Companion to Comics*, edited by Frank Bramlett et al., Routledge, 2017, pp. 390–398.

Modern Language Association of America, editor. *MLA Handbook*, 8th ed., The Modern Language Association of America, 2016.

Modern Language Association of America. "Works Cited: A Quick Guide." *The MLA Style Center*, 2019, https://is.gd/OIRn67

Moreno-García, Elena, et al. "Among the Mathematics Tasks, Math Courses and Math Exams: How's the Level of Student Anxiety toward Maths in a Private High School in Mexico?." *European Journal of Contemporary Education*, vol. 7(4), 2018, pp. 741–753, https://is.gd/c1XGq8

Muhammad, Craig. "'With Liberty and Justice for All'? A Look at Criminal Justice in America When the Blindfold Is Removed." *Journal of Prisoners on Prisons*, vol. 25, no. 1, 2016, pp. 53–61, https://is.gd/rxyk26

Nahai, Nathalie. *Webs of Influence: The Psychology of Online Persuasion*, 2nd ed., Pearson Education, 2017.

Nisbet, Jordan. "Overcoming Math Anxiety: 12 Evidence-Based Tips That Work." *Prodigy Math Blog*, 8 Mar. 2019, https://is.gd/tUBlVg

O'Dell, Kailan. "The Evolution of the Grand Piano." *Sono Music*, 2 Sept. 2014, https://is.gd/1uUXHF

OrionStarlancer. "Are Comics Literature?" *Comic Vine*, 29 Aug. 2010, https://is.gd/0rpn5O

Oxford University Press, editor. *New Oxford Style Manual*, 3rd ed., Oxford University Press, 2016.

Palmer, Louis J. "Death-Eligible Offenses." *Encyclopedia of Capital Punishment in the United States*, 2nd ed., McFarland & Company, 2008, pp. 141–142.

Petersen, Robert S. "The Return of Graphic Narratives for Adults." *Comics, Manga, and Graphic Novels: A History of Graphic Narratives*, Praeger, 2011, pp. 205–226, https://is.gd/JegDAw

Piwowar, Heather, et al. "The State of OA: A Large-Scale Analysis of the Prevalence and Impact of Open Access Articles." *PeerJ*, vol. 6, Feb. 2018, pp. 1–23, https://is.gd/bIJD5h

Pool, Gail. *Faint Praise: The Plight of Book Reviewing in America*, University of Missouri Press, 2007.

Potter, David. "Part 4: Roman Games." *The Victor's Crown: A History of Ancient Sport from Homer to Byzantium*, Oxford University Press, 2012, pp. 163–222, https://is.gd/Avr4oD

Prince, Stephen. *Digital Cinema*, Rutgers University Press, 2019.

Puchner, Walter, and Andrew Walker White. *Greek Theatre between Antiquity and Independence: A History of Reinvention from the Third Century BC to 1830*, Cambridge University Press, 2017, https://is.gd/wZtFqq

Pyrczak, Fred, and Maria Tcherni-Buzzeo. *Evaluating Research in Academic Journals: A Practical Guide to Realistic Evaluation*, 7th ed., Routledge, 2019.

Rawcliffe, Heather Joanne. *Lava-Water-Sediment Interaction: Processes, Products and Petroleum Systems* (Doctoral Dissertation). University of Glasgow, 2015, https://is.gd/ENxnUs

Regazzi, John J. *Scholarly Communications: A History from Content as King to Content as Kingmaker*, Rowman & Littlefield, 2015.

Riordan, Daniel G. *Technical Report Writing Today*, 10th ed., Wadsworth, 2014.

Roberts, Bruce D. "Ford Fiasco: Tracking the Rise and Fall of the Edsel in American Newspaper Archives." *Readex Report*, vol. 8, no. 3, Sept. 2013, https://is.gd/yELqpQ

Robinson, Antony, Meredith Lewin, and Margaret Lodder. *Systematic Bibliography: A Practical Guide to the Work of Compilation*, 4th ed., C. Bingley, 1979.

Satin, Morton. "The Chemistry and Health Benefits of Coffee." *Coffee Talk: The Stimulating Story of the World's Most Popular Brew*, Prometheus Books, 2011, pp. 65–88. *Library of Congress ISBN*, https://is.gd/4omg9w

Shaffer, Leah. "The Fear of Math: Five Strategies to Help Students Conquer Their Math Anxiety." *Scholastic Instructor*, vol. 124, no. 5, 2015, pp. 27–29.

Shoemaker, Greg. "Daiei: A History of the Greater Japan Motion Picture Company." *The Japanese Fantasy Film Journal*, vol. 12, 1979, pp. 10–15, https://is.gd/831XYa

Spatt, Brenda. *Writing from Sources*, 9th ed., Bedford/St. Martin's, 2016.

Speake, J., S. Edmondson, and H. Nawaz. "Everyday Encounters with Nature: Students' Perceptions and Use of University Campus Green Spaces." *Human Geographies – Journal of Studies and Research in Human Geography*, vol. 7(1), 2013, pp. 21–31, https://is.gd/chWnxx

Spiegelman, Art. *Maus: A Survivor's Tale Part 1: My Father Bleeds History*, Penguin Books, 1987, https://is.gd/NVJAm7

Spinelli, Martin. *Podcasting: The Audio Media Revolution*, Bloomsbury Academic, 2019.

Spiro, Rand J., et al. "Cognitive Flexibility, Constructivism, and Hypertext: Random Access Instruction for Advanced Knowledge Acquisition in Ill-Structured Domains." *Educational Technology*, vol. 31(5), 1991, pp. 24–33.

Spry, Adam. "Louis Riel: A Comic-Strip Biography." *Critical Survey of Graphic Novels: Independents and Underground Classics.*, edited by Bart Beaty, and Stephen Weiner, 2nd ed., Vol. 2, Salem Press, 2019, pp. 487–490.

Steiker, Carol S., and Jordan M. Steiker. "The Future of the American Death Penalty." *Courting Death: The Supreme Court and Capital Punishment*, The Belknap Press of Harvard University Press, 2016, pp. 255–289.

Stephens, Maria, et al. *Highlights from TIMSS and TIMSS Advanced 2015: Mathematics and Science Achievement of U.S. Students in Grades 4 and 8 and in Advanced Courses at the End of High School in an International Context.* Government Report, NCES 2017-002, 2016, https://is.gd/rDiPR6

Stogner, Maggie Burnette. *In the Executioner's Shadow: A Film about Justice, Injustice and the Death Penalty.* New Day Films, 2018, https://is.gd/zpnVsj

Sumner, David E. *The Magazine Century: American Magazines since 1900*, Peter Lang, 2010.

Tanaka, Minnie. *The Twelve Large Colour Prints of William Blake: A Study on Techniques, Materials and Context* (Doctoral Dissertation). Nottingham Trent University, 2008, https://is.gd/GZCxMc

Tanner, Lindsey. "Philadelphia's Soda Tax Has Reduced Soft-Drink Sales, Study Says, and Raised $130M for Preschool." *Chicago Tribune*, 14 May 2019, https://is.gd/WG94WP

Teufel, Simone, and Marc Moens. "Summarizing Scientific Articles: Experiments with Relevance and Rhetorical Status." *Computational Linguistics*, vol. 28, no. 4, 2002, pp. 409–445.

The Constitution Project. *Irreversible Error: Recommended Reforms for Preventing and Correcting Errors in the Administration of Capital Punishment.* The Constitution Project, 2014, https://is.gd/FcCI7P

The CUNY TV Foundation. "Yasmina Reza's "God of Carnage," with James Gandolfini, Marcia Gay Harden, Jeff Daniels, and Hope Davis." *The CUNY TV Foundation*, 24 Apr. 2009, https://is.gd/2fz2hI

The Gravitational Wave International Committee, et al. "Gravitational-Wave Astronomy in the 2020s and Beyond: A View across the Gravitational Wave Spectrum." *National Aeronautics and Space Administration (NASA) Goddard Space Flight Center*, 20 Mar. 2019, https://is.gd/v1Dy4h

The Understood Team. *Signs of Math Anxiety/Signs of Dyscalculia.* 2019, https://is.gd/EK3rqM

The University of Chicago Press, editor. *The Chicago Manual of Style*, 17th ed., The University of Chicago Press, 2017a.

The University of Chicago Press. "Chicago-Style Citation: A Quick Guide." *The Chicago Manual of Style Online*, 2017b, https://is.gd/uNmKlS

Tobias, Sheila, and Sheila Haag. "Math Anxiety and Gender." *Encyclopedia of Diversity in Education*, edited by James A. Banks, Vol. 3, SAGE Publications, Inc, 2012, pp. 1441–1444.

Tomasino Rodríguez, Vanesa. "Review of Mortal Doubt: Transnational Gangs and Social Order in Guatemala City." *European Review of Latin American and Caribbean Studies*, vol. 107, 2019, pp. 5–7, https://is.gd/4RlNzn

Turabian, Kate L. *A Manual for Writers of Research Papers, Theses, and Dissertations: Chicago Style for Students and Researchers*, Edited by Wayne C. Booth et al., 9th ed., The University of Chicago Press, 2018.

Vie, Stephanie, and Brandy Dieterle. "Minding the Gap: Comics as Scaffolding for Critical Literacy Skills in the Classroom." *Composition Forum*, vol. 33, 2016, https://is.gd/atJwAw

Vishton, Peter M. *Getting a Jump on Math – Without Math Anxiety*. 12, 2014, https://is.gd/swb0Uj

Von Drehle, David. "Execution in America." *Time*, vol. 185, no. 4, June. 2015, pp. 27–33, https://is.gd/Nf3rWG

Wallace, Aurora. *Newspapers and the Making of Modern America: A History*, Greenwood Press, 2005.

Wallraff, Barbara. *Your Own Words*, Counterpoint, 2004.

Wells, Liz, editor. *The Photography Reader: History and Theory*, 2nd ed., Routledge, 2019.

Wheelock, John Hall. *A Bibliography of Theodore Roosevelt*, Charles Scribner's Sons, 1920, https://is.gd/cs7IaQ

Wikimedia Foundation. "Classics Illustrated." *Wikipedia*, 16 Sept. 2019a, https://is.gd/P9S6aH

Wikimedia Foundation. "Comparison of Reference Management Software." *Wikipedia*, 13 Nov. 2019b, https://is.gd/C5st5N

Williams, Kevin. *Read All about It! A History of the British Newspaper*, Routledge, 2010.

Winkler, Anthony C., and Jo Ray McCuen. *Writing the Research Paper: A Handbook*, 8th ed., Thomson Wadsworth, 2012.

Yagcioglu, Ozlem. *The Positive Effects of Cognitive Learning Styles in ELT Classes*, vol. 1, no. 2, 2016, pp. 78–91, https://is.gd/zIWkdn

Young, Jamaal Rashad, and Jemimah Lea Young. "Young, Black, and Anxious: Describing the Black Student Mathematics Anxiety Research Using Confidence Intervals." *Journal of Urban Mathematics Education*, vol. 9, no. 1, 2016, pp. 79–93, https://is.gd/5M30Ir

Zerby, Chuck. *The Devil's Details: A History of Footnotes*, Simon & Schuster, Touchstone Book, 2003.

Zivot, Joel B. "The Absence of Cruelty Is Not the Presence of Humanness: Physicians and the Death Penalty in the United States." *Philosophy, Ethics, and Humanities in Medicine*, vol. 7, no. 1, 2012, pp. 7:13 1–4, https://is.gd/8K68Ou

INDEX

Made in United States
Troutdale, OR
08/30/2023

12499706R00091